CONTENTS

Library of Congress Cataloging-in-Publication Data

Names: O'Hara, Vincent P., [date] author.
Title: Heavy cruiser Prinz Eugen / Vincent P. O'Hara.
Other titles: Naval history 1042-1920
Description: Annapolis, MD : Naval Institute Press, [2022] | Series: Naval history special edition | Title from cover.
Identifiers: LCCN 2022003544 | ISBN 9781591148722 (paperback)
Subjects: LCSH: Prinz Eugen (Cruiser)--History.
Classification: LCC VA515.P75 O33 2022 | DDC 359.3/253--dc23/eng/20220127
LC record available at https://lccn.loc.gov/2022003544

INTRODUCTION

An aerial starboard bow view of the *Admiral Hipper*–class heavy cruiser *Prinz Eugen* underway in Gatún Lake, Panama on or around 15 March 1946. (U.S. Navy)

This *Naval History* Special Edition is about the German heavy cruiser *Prinz Eugen*. *Prinz Eugen*, one of three *Admiral Hipper*–class heavy cruisers, won distinction for several reasons. She participated in several famous operations, most notably as a companion to the battleship *Bismarck* in her doomed sortie into the North Atlantic in May 1941, and as part of the German task flotilla that forced the English Channel in February 1942. She survived mine, submarine, air, and surface attacks. She nearly wore out the barrels of her 20.3-cm (8-inch) main batteries supporting the German army against the inexorable Soviet advance into the Reich, participating in dozens of bombardment actions that are all but forgotten today. She was largest German warship to make it through the war intact and postwar became a commissioned vessel in the U.S. Navy. She weathered two atomic bomb tests largely undamaged, finally foundering at a remote Pacific atoll through neglect.

This *Naval History* Special Edition covers the design and career of *Prinz Eugen* and seeks to give context to her history with discussions of what similar designs were intended to do and how they fared. The performance of *Prinz Eugen*'s sisters, particularly *Admiral Hipper*, is particularly important in this regard. *Prinz Eugen*'s career offers an excellent window into many of the challenges that faced the German navy during World War II and insight into the strategic imperatives that dictated how Germany used its always-outnumbered surface fleet. *Prinz Eugen* was an innovative if not always successful design, but she succeeded when given a task. Her story is well worth telling.

CHRONOLOGY

23 April 1936: Laid down at Germaniawerft, Kiel, as "Schwere Kreuzer J."

22 August 1938: Launched and christened as the Schwere Kreuzer *Prinz Eugen* by the wife of the Hungarian regent, Admiral Nicholas Horthy.

1940

2 July: Struck by two small bombs in a Royal Air Force raid while fitting out at Kiel.

1 August: Commissioned.

August–November: Conducts trials near Kiel.

1941

January: Works up in the Baltic.

8 April: Departs Kiel for Gotenhafen.

22 April: Strikes a mine and suffers minor damage while en route to Kiel.

18 May: Sails from Gotenhafen to participate in planned Atlantic breakout with battleship *Bismarck*.

24 May: Engagement with *Hood* and *Prince of Wales*. She parts company with *Bismarck* that night to engage in independent mercantile warfare.

1 June: Cuts cruise short due to engine problems and returns to Brest.

2 July: Hit by bomb in RAF raid on Brest and suffers major damage.

July–December: In dock at Brest undergoing repairs.

15 December: Repairs completed.

1942

7 February: Trials completed.

11–13 February: In company with German flotilla, transits the English Channel.

21 February: Leaves home waters with *Admiral Scheer* for transfer to Norway.

23 February: Torpedoed by Royal Navy submarine *Trident* off Trondheim, Norway, and seriously damaged.

16 May: After emergency repairs, departs Trondheim for Kiel.

17 May: Defeats large attack by torpedo bombers south of Norway.

18 May: Arrives at Kiel.

May–October: In dock at Kiel.

20 October: Repairs completed.

November–December: Conducts trials and works up in the Baltic.

1943

9 January: In company with *Scharnhorst* attempts passage to Norway. Detected by the British en route and returns to Gotenhafen.

23 January: Makes second attempt to transfer to Norway with *Scharnhorst*, same results, returns to Gotenhafen.

February: Assigned to training squadron in the Baltic.

1944

February: Returns to active service in Baltic as part of 2nd Task Force.

19 June: Deploys to the Gulf of Finland to support Finns suffering heavy Soviet attacks.

20–21 August: Deploys against Soviet troops near Tukums on the Gulf of Riga to conduct shore bombardments.

13–18 September: Provides distant cover for German landings on Hogland Island.

21–25 September: With 2nd Task Force covers evacuations from the Gulf of Finland and Estonia.

10–15 October: With 2nd Task Force shells Soviet positions near Memel.

15 October: While returning to Gotenhafen, collides with *Leipzig* in the fog, nearly cutting the lightly armored cruiser in two.

7 November: Repairs completed.

20–21 November: Bombards Soviet targets on the Sworbe Peninsula, Estonia.

December: Enters dock to reline gun barrels.

1945

January: Dock work completed by the first week of January.

29–31 January: Supports German operations in Samland.

March: Performs fire-support missions around Gotenhafen, Danzig, and Tiegenhoff.

1 April: Hit by Soviet rocket in an air attack.

4 April: Engages in final shore bombardment.

13 April: Attacked at Swinemünde by RAF.

20 April: Arrives at Copenhagen.

9 May: Surrendered at Copenhagen.

24–26 May: Transferred to Wilhelmshaven under Royal Navy escort.

19 October: Ceded to the United States.

1946

13 January: Departs for Boston.

22 January: Arrives in Boston.

11 March: Departs for Pacific.

10 May: Arrives at Pearl Harbor.

1 July: At Bikini Atoll. Survives A-bomb test Able.

25 July: Survives A-bomb test Baker. Following these tests, she remains afloat without structural damage.

29 August: Decommissioned at Kwajalein Atoll.

21 December: Takes on a 35° list due to undetected intake of water.

22 December: Towed to Enubuj Reef, where she capsizes.

GERMANY AND TREATY CRUISERS

PRINZ EUGEN AND HER PEERS

The cruiser is a warship type with a long pedigree. It was conceived as a ship intended to sail outside the line of battle. It was faster than a line-of-battle ship, not as heavily armed or armored (if armored at all) but capable of independent action and dominating distant waters. Its classic functions consisted of reconnaissance, raiding enemy commerce, and protecting friendly traffic. Before the World War I the naval powers valued cruisers as expendable platforms that could show the flag on distant stations and protect national interests.

When World War I started there were four basic cruiser types:

- Light cruisers. These were 30-knot-plus vessels armed with torpedoes and guns of between 3.9 to 6-inch. They were very lightly armored, if at all. They generally served with the battle fleet as scouts and often led destroyer flotillas. They also acted as raiders or protected light forces.

- Protected cruisers. These were larger than light cruisers and not as fast. They generally had a lightly armored decks and 6-inch guns. By 1914 the type was becoming obsolete. They were mainly used to protect shipping and show the flag.

- Armored cruisers. These were large vessels generally capable of 25 knots and carrying main gun batteries ranging in size between 7.5-inch and 10-inch. They had protection against other cruisers' guns. In smaller navies they supplemented the line of battle by acting as "fast wings." They also served on foreign stations.

- Battle cruisers. They had the size and armament of a battleship, the speed of a light cruiser, and the armor of a protected cruiser. They were intended to serve as cruiser killers and as the fast wing of the battle line. This was a new type in 1914; only Great Britain, Germany, and Japan possessed battle cruisers.

(pictured above) German light cruiser of the *Magdeburg* class, probably *Strassburg*, pictured at sea in 1915. This class was built between 1910 and 1916 and was representative of the German light cruisers that fought hard, and with some success, in World War I. They displaced 5,280 tons, could make 27 knots, were lightly armored, and carried a dozen 10.5-cm quick-firing (QF) guns in single mounts. (NHHC)

Germany had a very strong cruiser force in 1914:

- 35 light cruisers (with four building); 19 were war losses

- 9 armored cruisers, of which 6 were lost

- 6 protected cruisers (all coast-defense vessels by 1914)

- 4 battle cruisers (with three building), of which 1 was lost

These vessels had an active war, fighting in numerous surface actions and engaging in epic cruises and destructive raiding expeditions. They established several traditions in the German navy, of fights against long odds, of success, and of courage and sacrifice. In general, while German cruisers enjoyed several victories in surface actions, such as the Battle of Coronel, generally they fought as the weaker force and suffered accordingly.

The post–World War I Treaty of Versailles reduced the German navy to a shadow of its former self and rendered coast defense its only valid mission. The cruiser force was limited to six vessels, with two in reserve. All were all more than fifteen years old. They could be replaced only at twenty years, and the size of their replacements was limited to 6,000 tons.

As the German navy stagnated under treaty constraints, warships continued to evolve in the navies of Great Britain, the United States, Japan, France, and Italy, as these navies quickly went from being victorious partners to potential rivals.

In some respects, the "heavy cruiser" of World War II seems to be a development of the armored cruiser of World War I, but this resemblance is superficial. In fact, the heavy cruiser was a product of the 1920 Washington Treaty. The treaty's intent was to constrain warship construction and prevent costly and dangerous arms races, such as the dreadnought-building race between Great Britain and Germany, which some saw as having been a contributing factor to the outbreak of World War I. The parties to the treaty—Great Britain, the United States, Japan, France, and Italy—agreed to limit the number of battleships, battle cruisers, and aircraft carriers. Total cruiser tonnage was unlimited, but size and armament were restricted to 10,000 tons and guns no larger than 8-inch. Although 10,000-ton cruisers armed with 8-inch guns and capable of speeds in excess of 30 knots did not exist before the treaty was signed, all the major navies of the time and some second-tier powers as well were soon building them. The first of the new "Treaty" heavy cruisers was commissioned in 1926. Up through the start of

The German armored cruiser *Yorck*. As a type, German armored cruisers suffered heavily; six of nine became war losses, most famously *Gneisenau* and *Scharnhorst* at the Battle of the Falklands. *Yorck*'s demise was not so spectacular: she was a victim of floating mines outside the mouth of the Jade in November 1914. She displaced 10,266 tons, could steam at 21 knots, and carried four 21-cm, ten 15-cm, and twelve 88-mm guns. Armored cruisers were too lightly armed and armored to face dreadnoughts, a fact graphically illustrated at the Falklands and Jutland. (NHHC)

German battle cruisers of World War I were fast, tough, powerful, and hard to sink. Arguably they were the best capital ships of the period. *Seidlitz* pictured here was commissioned in 1913. She survived very heavy damage at the 1914 Battle of Dogger Bank and at Jutland, making port despite shipping 5,300 tons of water. She displaced 28,500 tons, could steam at 28 knots, and was armed with ten 28-cm guns. (NHHC)

World War II nine nations constructed seventy-six heavy cruisers, as follows:

- Great Britain: *Kent, London, Norfolk,* and *York* classes (15). First February 1928, last July 1931

- United States: *Pensacola, Northampton, Portland, New Orleans, Wichita* (18). First December 1929, last February 1939

- France: *Duquesne, Suffren, Algérie* (7). First September 1926, last May 1932

- Italy: *Trento, Zara, Bolzano* (7). First December 1928, last August 1933

- Japan: *Furutaka, Nachi, Takao, Mogami, Tone* (17). First March 1926, last May 1939

- Germany: *Admiral Hipper* (3). First April 1939, last August 1940

- Soviet Union: *Krasnyi Kavkaz, Kirov, Maxim Gorkiy* (5). First January 1932, last June 1941

- Spain: *Canarias* (2). First May 1931, last April 1932

- Argentina: *Veinticinco de Mayo* (2). First August 1929, last September 1929

This list does not include the wartime U.S. Navy heavy cruisers of the *Baltimore*-class, as they were unbound by the Washington Treaty.

What function was a heavy cruiser supposed to serve? A December 1942 U.S. Naval Institute *Proceedings* article identified the role of the modern heavy cruiser: "First, she is a middle-sized warship, often serving as the capital ship where no battleships are to be had, and carrying out all jobs too minor or too dangerous for the battleship. Second, she is a scout and advance guard for the fleet. Third, she is a commerce destroyer. Her requisites are logically: (1) Size small enough to be produced in quantity, (2) speed enough to evade most battleships, (3) fighting power within these limits the highest possible, limited by nothing else." Thus: the function of the heavy cruiser was to act as a surrogate battleship and a light-cruiser killer, in addition to the traditional cruiser duties. Modern battleships faced each other in combat only twice.

The British heavy cruiser *Norfolk*. Commissioned in 1930, she had an active war career, participating in actions against *Bismarck* and *Scharnhorst* and serving in the Atlantic and Arctic. She displaced 10,035 tons, could steam at 31.5 knots, and carried eight 8-inch guns, along with a secondary battery of eight 4-inch QF antiaircraft guns. (NHHC)

"Washington cruisers," however, squared off against each other in nine actions.

- 27 November 1940, the Battle of Cape Spartivento. In this action the British heavy cruiser *Berwick*, part of a force that included a battleship, a battle cruiser, four light cruisers, and ten destroyers, faced an Italian squadron consisting of six heavy cruisers (*Pola*, *Fiume*, *Gorizia*, *Trieste*, *Trento*, and *Bolzano*), two battleships, and fourteen destroyers. Just two minutes after opening fire *Pola* hit *Berwick* from nearly 24,000 yards. The 8-inch shell exploded in *Berwick*'s Y-turret barbette, knocking its guns out of action. Another 8-inch round hit the British heavy cruiser fourteen minutes later, penetrated the upper and lower decks, and burst between the gun room and the Y-barbette shell handling room. On the Italian

side a destroyer was heavily damaged, by hits and splinters. Nevertheless, this action, fought for nearly an hour at long ranges, was indecisive.

- 25 December 1940, the Christmas Convoy Attack. In this action *Admiral Hipper*, on her first commerce-raiding cruise, came upon Convoy WS5A, carrying forty thousand troops and escorted by two light cruisers and *Berwick*, only temporarily repaired since her action the month before. In poor visibility and heavy seas *Hipper* attacked at dawn on 25 December. Between 0639 and 0714 the cruisers engaged in a running fight from approximately eight thousand yards. *Hipper* fired 185 20.3-cm rounds and hit the British cruiser four times before *Berwick* ran into a rain squall that separated the foes. *Hipper* knocked out *Berwick*'s X turret and caused flooding in two locations. The damage should have been worse,

USS *Wichita*, pictured in Scapa Flow in April 1942. She was the final American heavy cruiser design constrained by Washington Treaty limits and perhaps the best all-around expression of the type. (NHHC)

The French heavy cruiser *Foch* commissioned in 1931, the last of the four-ship *Suffren*-class. She was never tested in action before being scuttled at Toulon in November 1942. (NHHC)

but two German shells failed to explode. All of *Berwick*'s rounds missed although some of her tightly grouped patterns fell close enough to send splinters rattling on board the German cruiser. *Berwick* spent six months in dock fixing this damage and that inflicted on 27 November.

- 27 February 1942, the Battle of the Java Sea. Two Japanese heavy cruisers, *Nachi* and *Haguro*, were escorting an invasion convoy to Java along with two light cruisers and fourteen destroyers when they were confronted by two Allied heavy cruisers (*Houston* and *Exeter*), three light cruisers, and nine destroyers. In an extended battle fought at long ranges *Nachi* landed a shell on *Exeter* that

exploded in the B boiler room, knocking six of eight boilers off-line. The battle eventually ended after seven and a quarter hours when *Nachi* and *Haguro* torpedoed and sank the two Dutch light cruisers. The Japanese heavy cruisers fired 1,619 8-inch shells and got five hits from ranges as long as 22,000 yards. Three of these hits were duds, however. The count of shells expended by *Houston* and *Exeter* is not known; neither one scored a direct hit, but *Houston* lightly damaged *Naka* when splinters from a near miss severed an antenna.

- 1 March 1942, The Battle of Sunda Strait. *Houston* and a light cruiser attempted to escape the waters north of Java, only to run into another

The Italian heavy cruiser *Zara*. She was 12 percent oversized, with a standard displacement of 11,680 tons. For the extra weight she had good protection and speed and armament equal to those of all other Treaty types. She and two sisters, *Fiume* and *Polo*, had active careers until being ambushed and sunk by British battleships in the night action off Cape Matapan in March 1941. (NHHC)

Italy's heavy cruisers of the 1st and 3rd Divisions, here sailing together in formation at the Battle of Calabria, formed a powerful force that the British could oppose in the Mediterranean only with capital ships. (Maurizo Brescia Collection)

Japanese invasion convoy that included in its escort the heavy cruisers *Mogami* and *Mikuma*, a light cruiser, and nine destroyers. The Allied force was low on ammunition and shot away all of it before being overwhelmed by destroyer torpedoes. The Japanese heavy cruisers as well fired powerful torpedo barrages at the Allied ships, but the weapons ran past their targets and sank four friendly vessels in the invasion convoy.

• 1 March 1942, Action South of Borneo. *Exeter* and two destroyers tried to flee the Java Sea but were cornered by *Nachi*, *Haguro*, *Ashigara*, and *Myoko*, supported by four destroyers. The damaged British cruiser's top speed was 16 knots, and she was down to 20 percent of her ammunition. During the battle the Japanese avoided Allied destroyer torpedoes and hit *Exeter* once again in the

boiler room. As she slowed to a stop, more 8-inch shells rained down. The Japanese also launched twenty-five torpedoes at *Exeter*, but only one hit. The Japanese sank the entire Allied force.

• 9 August 1942, the Battle of Savo Island. In this, the largest heavy-cruiser surface action of the war, five Japanese heavy cruisers (*Chokai Aoba*, *Kinugasa*, *Furutaka*, and *Kako*), along with two light cruisers and a destroyer, came roaring down New Georgia Sound to attack an American invasion force off Guadalcanal. This amphibious force was defended by four American and one Australian heavy cruisers: *Chicago*, *Vincennes*, *Astoria*, *Quincy*, and *Canberra*. With shell fire and torpedoes the Japanese damaged *Chicago* and sank the other four Allied cruisers, at the cost of relatively light damage inflicted on *Chokai* by an 8-inch shell. This

If the Italians cheated with their designs, the Japanese cheated better. *Takeo* displaced 13,400 tons after being reconstructed in 1940. She also carried a very heavy battery of sixteen 24-inch "Long Lance" torpedoes. (NHHC)

The heavy cruiser USS *San Francisco* returns to Mare Island, California, after the November 1942 Naval Battle of Guadalcanal. The white circles indicate where she was hit by shell fire. (NHHC)

action demonstrated the lethality of the class as well as its fragility.

- 11 October 1942, the Battle of Cape Esperance. In the continuing battle to control the waters surrounding Guadalcanal the Japanese heavy cruisers *Aoba*, *Kinugasa*, and *Furutaka* were approaching the island with two destroyers to bombard its airfield. They ran into *San Francisco*, *Salt Lake City*, two light cruisers, and five destroyers. The American force enjoyed surprise and crossed the Japanese "T." Their gunfire severely damaged *Aoba*, sank *Furutaka*, and more lightly damaged *Kinugasa*. *Kinugasa* landed several shells on *San Francisco* and moderately damaged her.

- 27 March 1943, the Battle of Komandorski Islands. An American force that included *Salt Lake City*, a light cruiser, and four destroyers intercepted a Japanese supply convoy escorted by *Nachi*, *Maya*, two light cruisers, and three destroyers. The heavy cruisers on both sides delivered long-range hits and *Salt Lake City* was in distress when the Japanese, low on fuel and ammunition, broke off.

- 25 October 1944, the Battle of Surigao Strait. Nineteen months passed before heavy cruisers once again faced each other, in this mainly battleship ac-tion. *Louisville*, *Portland*, *Minneapolis*, the Australian *Shropshire*, six battleships, and twenty-six destroyers confronted a Japanese flotilla that included *Mogami*,

A painting by the Italian artist Claudius depicting the Battle of Cape Esperance. Unfortunately, he depicts more modern cruisers than actually participated in the battle. (NHHC)

Nachi, and *Ashigara*, two battleships, a light cruiser, and ten destroyers. *Mogami* absorbed a staggering amount of damage but survived the battle, only to be sunk in air attacks the next day.

Of these engagements of Washington Treaty cruisers versus other "Washington cruisers," only Java Sea, Savo Island, and Cape Esperance were major actions with important results. However, this does not mean that heavy cruisers did not see much action and take heavy casualties.

Excluding vessels lost through surrender or capture following surrender, forty—more than half the heavy cruisers built—were sunk during World War II by enemy action. Of these forty, only seven were sunk in cruiser-versus-cruiser actions and thirteen more in surface actions.

- Great Britain—5 of 15: two to aircraft, two by surface action, one by commando attack
- United States—7 of 18: one by aircraft, one by submarine, five by surface action

Thus, there were six ways heavy cruisers were sunk in World War II:

- Aircraft: 14
- Surface action: 13
- Submarine: 6
- Scuttling to prevent capture: 4
- Commando attacks: 2
- Shore defenses: 1.

The German *Blücher* was the only heavy cruiser sunk by shore defenses trying to rush the fortifications defending Oslo. (Wiki Commons)

By nation, losses break down as follows:

- France—4 of 7: all scuttled to prevent capture.
- Germany—2 of 3: one to shore batteries and torpedoes, one to aircraft
- Japan—17 of 17: nine by aircraft, four by submarines, three by surface action, one by commando attack
- Italy—5 of 7: one by aircraft, one by submarines, three by surface action

Trying to assess the qualities of various designs is an interesting exercise but ultimately an unreliable predictor of how any given ship performed in battle. Intangibles such as crew quality and training, leadership, relative position, the weather gage and weather generally, mechanical reliability, surprise, ammunition reliability, mission, and plain old luck trump theoretical rate of fire, muzzle velocity, or armor thickness and distribution. The most cursory examination of cruisers in combat will reveal this. That said, the following table rates the most modern Treaty cruisers of each nation by the following factors:

1. Main battery (weight of shell/minute)
2. Armor
3. Speed
4. Endurance
5. Reliability
6. Machinery dispersal
7. Electronics
8. Torpedo armament

In terms of this comparison, *Prinz Eugen* does not shine. Her gunnery scores high, her armor below average, her endurance poor, and her speed average. These qualities are all the more remarkable in that *Prinz Eugen*'s designers did not even attempt to adhere to the Treaty standards. The cruiser's standard displacement was 14,271 tons. With so much more weight to work with, they should have made her superior to the heavy cruisers of other nations: yet she clearly was not. In some respects, the designers took chances that did not work out as planned, the high-pressure propulsion machinery being the primary example. Her electronics were very good, and her fire control proved itself in action. She scored hits in both her surface engagements, and *Hipper* had a similar record of success. Nonetheless, given that she was the last of the European heavy cruisers to be designed and should have benefited from the experiences of other nations, not to mention being so overweight, her design was in some respects a failure.

However, *Prinz Eugen* was a powerful ship and a deadly foe. In her career she faced battleships, destroyers, motor torpedo boats, submarines, aircraft, and shore batteries. She was damaged by mines, submarines, and aircraft. She did damage to enemy battleships, destroyers, aircraft, and land units. She was a powerful and handsome ship. Her career serves as an example of what the German navy did right and what it did wrong. She was an asset to her service and to her nation, and a study of her history is interesting as well as rewarding.

Table 1.1 Comparisons

CLASS	N	B	A	A %	E	S	D	R	EL	T	O/A
NORFOLK	BR	11.9	1060	11	9	32	NO	(+)	0	8	18
WICHITA	US	14	1473	14	10	33	NO	(+)	(+)	0	25
ALGÉRIE	FR	11.4	2035	20	8.7	31	NO	0	(-)	6	14
TAKAO	JP	12.7	2368	18	7.5	34	NO	0	(-)	16++	22
ZARA	IT	10.8	2688	23	6	32	YES	0	(-)	0	14
PRINZ EUGEN	GE	13.7	2140	15	5.1	32	YES	(-)	(+)	12+	21

N = NATION

B = BROADSIDE = POUNDS/ METAL/MINUTE (000) INCLUDING SECONDARY BATTERIES. AT PUBLISHED RATES OF FIRE

A = TOTAL TONNAGE OF ARMOR IN DESIGN

A% = ARMOR AS A PERCENTAGE OF TOTAL DISPLACEMENT

E = NAUTICAL MILES RANGE (000) AT 15 KNOTS

S = KNOTS ROUNDED DOWN TO THE NEAREST WHOLE NUMBER

D = DISPERSION OF POWER PLANT

R = RELIABILITY OF POWER PLANT (+) IS GOOD, 0 IS AVERAGE, (-) IS POOR

EL = ELECTRONICS (AT TIME WHEN WAR STARTED)

T = TORPEDO ARMAMENT IN TUBES + INDICATES RELOADS OR SUPERIOR TYPE ++ INDICATES RELOADS AND SUPERIOR TYPE

O/A = OVERALL RANKING

Prinz Eugen in 1940, sailing to conduct trials during her working-up period. Her fine lines and powerful appearance are striking. (U.S. Naval Institute photo archive)

Cruisers in Action

One last way to compare the heavy cruisers of various nations is to tabulate how they did in surface actions. This table lists the surface actions the heavy cruisers of the various nations participated in, whether they inflicted damage in said action, and whether they suffered damage.

Although they fought fewer actions, by this measure the *Admiral Hipper*–class cruisers of Germany acquitted themselves well.

Table 1.2 Summary of Cruiser Surface Actions

NATION	ACTIONS	INFLICTED DAMAGE**	RECEIVED DAMAGE	TOTAL LOST
GREAT BRITAIN*	12	5	6	2
USA	11	9	7	5
FRANCE	1	0	0	0
JAPAN	15	14	8	3
ITALY	6	3	1	3
GERMANY***	5	5	2	0

* INCLUDES FOUR ACTIONS INVOLVING AUSTRALIAN HEAVY CRUISERS

** INDICATES DAMAGE BY HEAVY CRUISERS ON ANY TYPE OF SHIP DURING THE ACTION

*** EXCLUDES ARMORED SHIPS (POCKET BATTLESHIPS) LATER DESIGNATED AS HEAVY CRUISERS

PRINZ EUGEN

DESIGN, SPECIFICATIONS, AND CONSTRUCTION

Prinz Eugen, 20 August 1938. The crowds have gathered and are waiting for the dignitaries to arrive before the ship is launched down the slip. (U.S. Naval Institute photo archive)

Prinz Eugen afloat. Notice that the anchor that was hanging to starboard in the prior image has now been dropped, and a pair of tugboats are preventing the stern from swinging. The launching basin was a tight fit, and the launch was carefully controlled to prevent any embarrassing or costly accidents. (U.S. Naval Institute photo archive)

DESIGN

The Versailles Treaty banned Germany from building heavy cruisers, but this did not stop the German naval staff from closely following foreign developments. As Grand Admiral Eric Raeder stated in September 1934, "Think what one will of the 20.3-cm/10,000 tonne cruiser, the fact remains that other sea-powers have it, and our own 15-cm/6,000 tonne cruisers will be out-classed." In planning a heavy cruiser, the German naval staff aimed for a ship superior to the best foreign types, capable of high speed and having sufficient endurance to operate in the North Atlantic. The major uncertainties they pondered were whether to arm the vessel with 19-cm (7.5-inch) or 20.3-cm (8-inch) guns and whether to utilize diesel or steam propulsion.

The navy decided to build heavy cruisers in October 1934 and placed orders for two ships that month. Detailed planning commenced in April 1935, the month after Hitler renounced the Versailles Treaty.

The intent was to build the best heavy cruiser in the world, but the result was a design that ended up displacing nearly 50 percent more than its French, British, and American rivals, whose designers had all basically complied with the 10,000-ton limit. Moreover, Germany did not benefit from its disregard of treaty limitation as it might have. Naval staff made some decisions that compromised the design's effectiveness. The most telling was the use of a sophisticated but unproven high-pressure steam propulsion system. This did not deliver the range originally anticipated, and the boilers were complicated. If they were not handled correctly, they could boil dry in a few minutes. In operations, the ship's engines proved cranky and subject to breakdown. In contrast, the class had sophisticated and effective fire control and the best electronics suite of any cruiser afloat at the time. Their weapons worked well, as they repeatedly demonstrated in operations. Their armor scheme was never really tested in combat. *Blücher*, the second of the class, was sunk by shore batteries and a torpedo, but her fate was more a function of conditions, incomplete training, and poor decisions rather than of any design flaws. Finally, whatever else can be said, the *Admiral Hipper*–class heavy cruisers were handsome ships.

Prinz Eugen, or "Heavy Cruiser I," was the third ship in the *Hipper* class. Her contract was placed with Krupp Germaniawerft at Kiel on 16 November 1935, and the first keel sections were laid down on 23 April 1936. The hull was launched on 22 August 1938, christened by the wife of the Hungarian admiral and head of state Miklós Horthy. Adolf Hitler attended the launching, which was a politically charged event because the government had elected to name the cruiser after a famous Austrian general, in part to establish a connection between the military traditions and heritages of the extinct Habsburg state and modern Germany.

PRINZ EUGEN'S ARMAMENT

As launched, *Prinz Eugen* carried eight 20.3-cm guns in four twin turrets; twelve 10.5-cm, high-angle guns in six

Admiral Hipper–class heavy cruiser. Forecastle deck showing turrets. (NHHC)

twin mountings; twelve 37-mm guns in six twin mountings; eight 20-mm single-mounted guns; and twelve 533-mm torpedo tubes in four triple mounts.

The 20.3-cm (8-inch) SKC/34 60-calibre gun was a new design produced by Krupp. The superfiring turrets (B and C) had 7-meter range finders and weighed 289 tons. A and D turrets weighed 274 tons. The gun's basic characteristics were:

- Training gear rate: 8°/second
- Elevation rate: 8°/second
- Maximum elevation: 37°
- Firing cycle: 12 seconds
- Shell weight (lbs/kg): 269 / 122
- Muzzle velocity (fps/ms): 3,035 / 925
- Maximum range (yds/m): 36,680 / 33,540 (at 37°)

Ammunition was 320 HE nose fuze, 320 HE with tail fuze, and 320 AP for armored targets.

Secondary Guns

The secondary, or heavy antiaircraft, armament consisted of the 10.5-cm SKC/33 65-calibre gun. The total mounting weight was 29.13 tons. This was the standard weapon for all larger German warships. Its basic characteristics were:

- Training speed: 8°/second
- Elevation rate:12°/second
- Maximum elevation: 80°
- Firing cycle: 3 seconds
- Shell weight (lbs/kg): 33.3 / 15.1
- Muzzle velocity (fps/ms): 2,953 / 900
- Maximum range (yds/m): 19,360 / 17,700 at 48°

Ammunition supply was 6,200 shells with time fuze for aerial targets and 240 tracer rounds.

The antiaircraft battery as designed was strong for the time, but wartime experience showed it to be inadequate; it was supplemented as the war went on. As designed and launched, the ship's major close-range antiaircraft gun was the 37-mm L/83 C30 gun. Its basic characteristics were:

- Shell weight (lbs/kg): 1.636 / 0.742
- Muzzle velocity (fps/ms): 3,281 / 1,000
- Ceiling at 90° (ft/m): 15,750 / 4,800
- Maximum range (yds/m): 7,100 / 6,500
- Rate of fire: 160/barrel/minute (80 in practice)

The 20-mm L/65 Model C30 Oerlikon was a popular Swiss design used by the Americans, the British, the Italians, and the Germans, among others. In German service its characteristics were:

- Shell weight (lbs/kg): 0.2714 / 0.1231
- Muzzle velocity (fps/ms): 2,740 / 835
- Rate of fire: 280 rounds/minute
- Ceiling at 90° (ft/m): 10,000 / 3,050
- Maximum range (yds/m): 4,800 / 4,390

As designed, the ship carried approximately 4,000 37-mm and 24,000 20-mm rounds.

As the war progressed, the single 20-mm guns were exchanged for twin and then quadruple mountings. For the Channel Dash operation *Prinz Eugen* received an extra five quadruple mountings and then two more quadruples, at Kiel later in 1942. By 1944 she had two 37-mm twins, nine 40-mm singles, two 20-mm twins, and six 20-mm quadruple mountings. By January 1944 she carried seventeen single 40-mm and no 37-mm guns.

GUNS

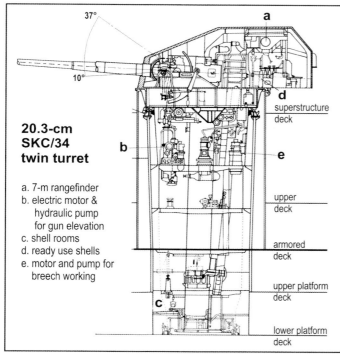

20.3-cm SKC/34 twin turret

a. 7-m rangefinder
b. electric motor & hydraulic pump for gun elevation
c. shell rooms
d. ready use shells
e. motor and pump for breech working

superstructure deck

upper deck

armored deck

upper platform deck

lower platform deck

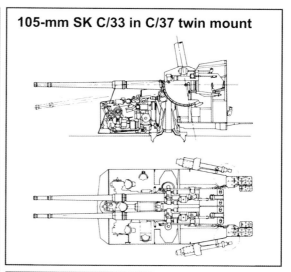

105-mm SK C/33 in C/37 twin mount

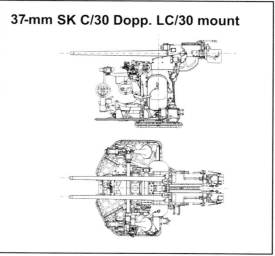

37-mm SK C/30 Dopp. LC/30 mount

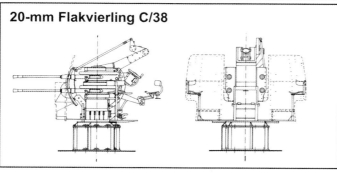

20-mm Flakvierling C/38

(Created by the Author)

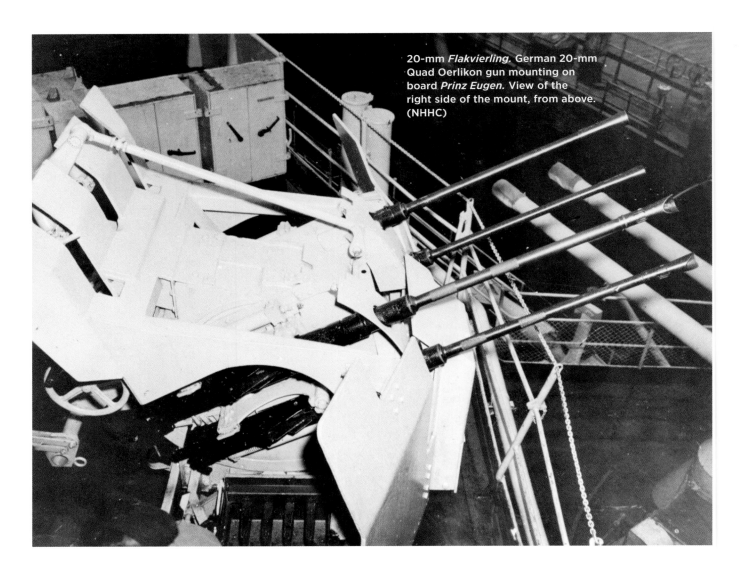

20-mm *Flakvierling.* German 20-mm Quad Oerlikon gun mounting on board *Prinz Eugen.* View of the right side of the mount, from above. (NHHC)

ARMOR ARRANGEMENTS

(in mm)

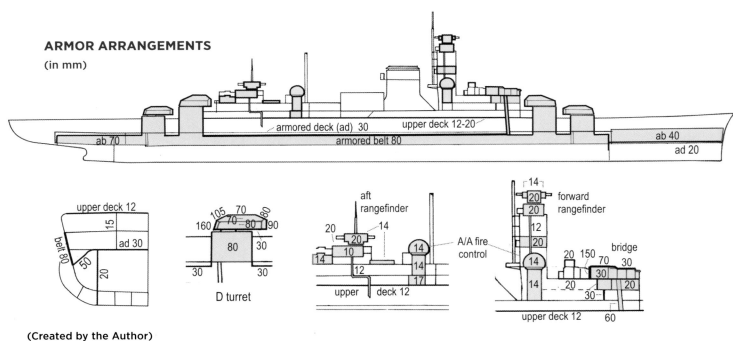

armored deck (ad) 30   upper deck 12-20

ab 70   armored belt 80   ab 40
ad 20

upper deck 12
15
belt 80
ad 30
50
20

105 70
160 70 80 80 90
80
30   30

D turret

aft rangefinder
20   14
14   10   14
14
12   17
upper deck 12

A/A fire control

14
20
forward rangefinder
20
12
20
14
14
20 150 bridge
70 30
14   20 30   20
30
upper deck 12   60

(Created by the Author)

Torpedoes

Prinz Eugen carried twelve 533-mm torpedoes in her tubes and a dozen more in containers located on either side of the funnel. These were Type G-7 torpedoes, which had a speed of 44 knots for a range of 5,800 meters, 40 knots for 7,000 meters, and 30 knots at ranges up to 12,000 meters. The explosive charge was 280 kg of TNT.

ARMOR

Prinz Eugen's protection scheme consisted of an armor belt for horizonal protection and two armored decks for vertical protection. Sensitive areas such as command, fire control, and gun turrets were also armored. Armor thickness varied depending on the location and the area being protected:

- Belt: 20–80 mm (0.79 to 3.15 inches)
- Upper deck: 12–25 mm (0.47 to 0.98 inches)
- Armor deck: 20–40 mm (0.79 to 1.57 inches)
- Turrets: 60–160 mm (2.36 to 6.3 inches)

The main belt extended in its full thickness of 80 cm from frame 26, just aft of turret D, to frame 164, forward of turret A. The after end was protected by 70 mm of armor and the forward end by 40 mm, except for the very stem, which had 20 mm of protection. The belt sloped 12.5 degrees from the vertical and was 3.75 to 3.85 m tall, with 0.75 m extending below the waterline.

The main horizontal protection consisted of an armored upper deck of 12–20 mm for most of its extent, from the barbettes for A and D turrets, with a small area amidships over the boiler spaces with 25 mm. The armored deck was 30 mm in thickness for most of its extent, from frame 6 aft to frame 163 forward, except for 20 mm covering the forecastle and small areas of 40-mm armor over the magazine spaces.

The barbettes had 80 mm of armor, and the conning tower with the bridge and control stations was protected with 150-mm armor. The main range finder, the control position, and the admiral's bridge had 20-mm side protection. The four flak-director towers had 14-mm plating, and the various control positions had vertical and horizontal splinter protection ranging from 10 to 30 mm in thickness. The turrets each had a face of 160-mm, a top of 70-mm, and sides of 70- and 80-mm armor. The armor type was Krupp "Whn/a" nickel steel and was riveted to bulkheads, longitudinals, and the skin of the ship.

MACHINERY

Naval staff elected to power their heavy cruisers with high-pressure steam. They made this choice hoping for better fuel economy and extended range, because higher pressures would lead to smaller boilers and less piping and hence give safety and damage-control advantages. The basic arrangements consisted of twelve boilers situated in three spaces. The boilers were ultra-high-pressure 58–85 atmospheres forced draft, 35 t/h steam to a maximum of 50t/h. The main engines were a triple-shaft arrangement. They consisted of three sets of single-reduction geared turbines of Brown-Boveri design. Each turbine developed 44,000 hp. There were two main engine rooms and three electrical plants

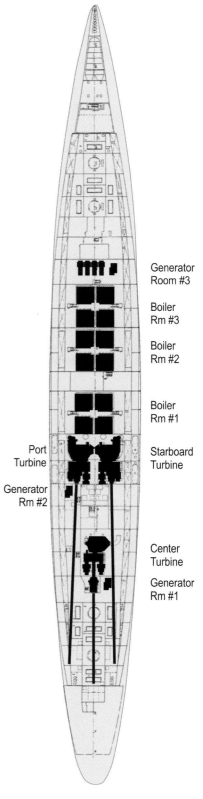

Generator Room #3

Boiler Rm #3

Boiler Rm #2

Boiler Rm #1

Port Turbine

Starboard Turbine

Generator Rm #2

Center Turbine

Generator Rm #1

(Created by the Author)

that had, in total, four diesel generators, three at 150 kW and one at 350 kW, and five turbo-generators, four at 460 kW and one at 230 kW, for a total capacity of 2,870 kW of AC at 220–230V.

RADAR AND SENSORS

When launched *Prinz Eugen* carried a sophisticated set of electronics and detection devices. She had enlarged range-finder towers, one aft and one on the foretop for the FuMo (Funkmess-Ortung) 27 direction finder

FuMo 27
Range: 13 nm
Accuracy: ± 70 m and ± 5°
Wavelength: 81.5 m
Frequency: 368 MHz
Output: 8 kW

and active-ranging sets. (German radar designations were changed in 1943, and the ultimate designations are used here.) Each set had a 2 x 4-meter mattress-type antenna. She also had on the foretop an FuMB 4 "Samos," a Funkmess-Erkennung passive radar detector designed to intercept enemy radar transmissions in the decametric range.

Although their technology was advanced, the Germans lacked an effective radar doctrine. German success with radar detection devices led to the

Prince Eugene of Savoy

Prinz Eugen von Savoyen, or, François-Eugène de Savole, or Prince Eugene of Savoy, was born in Paris in 1663, son of Olympia Mancini, Countess of Soissons, native of Rome (and niece of Cardinal Mazarin), and of Prince Eugène-Maurice of Savoy, at the time part of the Kingdom of Sardinia. Eugène-Maurice was a prominent general in the service of King Louis XIV of France His son would have followed him into the French army, except that the king refused his service because of a scandal involving his mother (of whom it was hinted that she poisoned her husband when Prinz Eugen was only ten and then threatened the king himself). That a German warship should be named after an Italian nobleman and son of a French general might seem strange at first take. In fact, after the disgrace of his mother Eugen traveled to Austria and entered Habsburg service, gaining fame after defeating the Ottomans at the Battle of Zenta in 1697 and becoming the scourge of the French in the War of the Spanish Succession. He was one of the great figures of the late 17th and early 18th centuries and a hero of the Austrian Empire.

After Germany annexed Austria in March 1938 the German navy acted to claim a share of the Austro-Hungarian naval tradition. "Heavy Cruiser I," which was on the slips, was designated to be named *Tegetthoff*, after the Austrian admiral who defeated the Italians in the 1866 Battle of Lissa and after one of the Austro-Hungarian

dreadnought battleships that served in World War I. However, by this time Italy was a major German ally, and to avoid offending Mussolini, the name *Prinz Eugen* was selected instead, as the third ship in the *Admiral Hipper*–class. This is how a German warship came to be named after the Italian son of a French general.

Prinz Eugen. Portrait unattributed, Flemish school, early 18th century.

Indicators for the FuMo 26, located in the top of the main gun director of *Prinz Eugen*, soon after V-E Day. (NHHC)

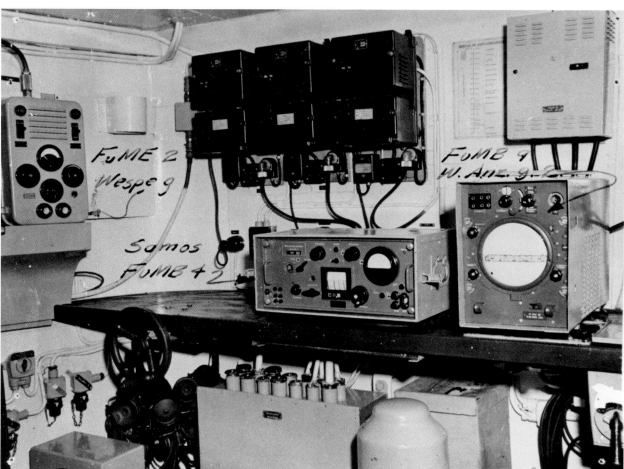

Interior of room in top of the main battery director, soon after V-E Day, showing FuMB 4 ("Samos") search receivers, part of the FuME 2 ("Wespe G") IFF, and various auxiliary panels. (NHHC)

false assumption that the British would be equally adept at picking up German transmissions. Thus, the Germans' use of detection and ranging sets was strictly limited during operations, negating most of the effectiveness of their devices.

During a refit after her February 1942 return to Germany, *Prinz Eugen*'s foretop FuMo 26 range finder was topped by an additional unit, above the 2 x 4-meter mattress and below the slightly smaller "Timor" frame, both bearing in the same direction, while the screen of the foretop platform carried passive "Sumatra" antennas, bearing in all four directions. *Prinz Eugen* was, moreover, unique in having a special height finder set with an aerial consisting of two rectangular frames that could be switched in elevation. The left one carried active dipoles, the right passive "butterfly" dipoles with vertical polarization. This may have been an experimental set for air search or for AA fire control.

When she was taken over by the United States, *Prinz Eugen* had a FuMo 26 on the foretop, a FuMo 81 at the foremast truck, a FuMo 25 on a platform abaft the mainmast, and an FuMo 23 as the after range finder. *Prinz Eugen* also carried a sophisticated hydrophone system called the *Gruppenhorchgerüt* (GHG). This consisted of two groups of sixty receivers in Compartment X. Each group was connected to a highly trained operator. This system detected the approach of *Hood* and *Prince of Wales* at 32,000 meters.

FIRE CONTROL

In the main batteries the ship carried four 7-meter range finders, in the foretop, the after fire-control position, and in B and C turrets. There was also a 6-meter range finder in the forward fire-control position. At night, fire control was conducted by four night-target "columns" on each side of the forward command post on the bridge. These positions were equipped with specialized light-gathering optics.

Turrets and guns could be fired individually. The range finders were linked to forward and aft main-battery plotting rooms (or control centers). The C/38 K fire-control computers continuously received the range from the range finders and displayed it on graphic time charts. Range rate (the rate of change of range over time) was calculated from the slope of a range-time graph and put into the computer. The computer then

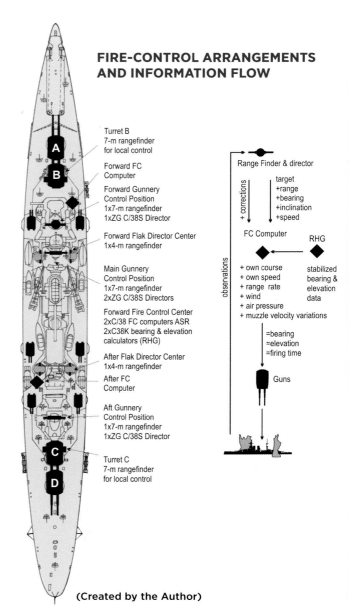

FIRE-CONTROL ARRANGEMENTS AND INFORMATION FLOW

Turret B
7-m rangefinder
for local control

Forward FC
Computer

Forward Gunnery
Control Position
1x7-m rangefinder
1xZG C/38S Director

Forward Flak Director Center
1x4-m rangefinder

Main Gunnery
Control Position
1x7-m rangefinder
2xZG C/38S Directors

Forward Fire Control Center
2xC/38 FC computers ASR
2xC38K bearing & elevation
calculators (RHG)

After Flak Director Center
1x4-m rangefinder

After FC
Computer

Aft Gunnery
Control Position
1x7-m rangefinder
1xZG C/38S Director

Turret C
7-m rangefinder
for local control

Range Finder & director
target
+range
+bearing
+inclination
+speed

+ corrections

observations

FC Computer   RHG

+ own course   stabilized
+ own speed   bearing &
+ range rate   elevation
+ wind   data
+ air pressure
+ muzzle velocity variations

=bearing
=elevation
=firing time

Guns

(Created by the Author)

calculated the range and deflection and transmitted that information to the gun-control units. There were also inputs for wind speed and direction, own course and speed, and target course and speed. There were three command posts, and each turret had auxiliary gear to enable fire to be maintained in the event of a breakdown in the main plotting rooms or a rupture in the cable connectors.

The *Prinz Eugen* was equipped with two stabilizing units, Rw Hw-Geber C/38 tilt-correction devices. These supplied stabilized bearing and elevation values to compensate for pitch, roll, and changes of own course. This allowed the guns to maintain continuous aim and to engage two targets simultaneously. Guns elevated

Prinz Eugen as completed. She was a remarkably handsome ship, with fine but powerful lines. The resemblance to the battleship *Bismarck* is striking. (U.S. Naval Institute photo archive)

- 697.18-ft / 212.5-meter overall length (after modification)

- 654.53-ft / 199.5-meter waterline length

- 71.85-ft / 21.9-meter maximum beam

- 26.08-ft / 7.95-meter operational draft

- 20.90-ft / 6.37-meter design draft

- 14,271 tons design

- 16,277 tons standard

- 18,960 tons operational

- Eight 20.3-cm (8-inch) SKC/34 60-calibre guns in four turrets

- Twelve 10.5-cm (4-inch) SKC/33 65-calibre guns in six mountings

- Twelve 37-mm L/83 C30 70-calibre guns in six mountings

- Eight 20-mm L/65 Model C30 Oerlikons in eight mountings

- Fuel oil 1,460 tons as designed, 3,250 maximum

- Speed 32 knots at 110,000 shp.

- Theoretical endurance at 3,400m³ load oil (4,300 tons)

- 2,050 nm at 32 knots (64 hours)

- 5,500 nm at 18 knots (305 hours)

- 6,100 nm at 15 knots (400 hours)

automatically but were hand-trained as ordered. The Rw Hw-Gebers fired the guns at the optimum point, allowing for roll and yaw. Each plotting room was manned by eight men. There was also a land-target computer in the forward plotting room. This allowed for the bombardment of unseen land targets if the bearing and distance of the target relative to a point visible from the ship was known.

In action the first gunnery officer normally exercised control from the foretop using the range finder located there. Other gunnery officers manned the plotting rooms ready to assume control should circumstances require. In daylight actions, initial range determination was made by one of the range finders or by averaging the value of the distances of all four range finders. There were also two 80-cm radar installations, one on the foretop and the other on the cupola of the after control post. Ranges could be taken from these sets and then passed on by telephone.

Antiaircraft fire control used the Type SL-8 finder. There were two antiaircraft plotting rooms, linked to transmitting and switching stations. They had their own fire-control computers fore and aft, with computers for the starboard and port sides. These calculated deflection, azimuth, elevation, and roll angles and determined the appropriate time setting on the shell fuzes.

Torpedoes were aimed using different night and day directors. These were equipped with two sights in the forward fire-control positions and one aft. Each set of tubes also had aiming optics.

CREW

At full strength under wartime conditions the ship's company consisted of 51 officers and 1,548 other ranks.

Prinz Eugen's crew cleaning D turret's 8-inch guns. (U.S. Naval Institute photo archive)

The ship's carpenters muster on station. (U.S. Naval Institute photo archive)

For Operation *Rheinübung*, *Prinz Eugen* carried 64 officers, 76 warrant officers, 408 NCOs, and 852 other ranks for a total of 1,400 men. She also carried prize crews and intelligence personnel. The ship's company was organized into ten divisions:

> **Divisions 1-4: Seaman branch, gunners, fire control, magazine and shell rooms, and senior officers**
>
> **Divisions 5-7: Engine room and damage-control personnel**
>
> **Division 8: Gun and torpedo mechanics, armorers, aircraft personnel**
>
> **Division 9: Communications and radar, coxswains**
>
> **Division 10: Administrative and services including cooks, paymaster, tailors, barbers, stewards, master at arms, boatswains, musicians, civilians, other specialists**

In comparison, a U.S. *New Orleans*–class heavy cruiser had about 950 men. Less than 800 men crewed a *British County*–class cruiser. An Italian *Trento*-class ship had roughly the same size crew as a British County.

AIRCRAFT

Prinz Eugen was designed to carry three catapult-launched Arado Ar 196 seaplanes. The two-man crew included a Luftwaffe pilot and a naval officer as navigator/gunner. The Arado 196 had a top speed of 192 mph, or 167 knots. Its range was 580 nautical miles. It carried two wing-mounted 20-mm cannons and two 7.9-mm machine guns. Its load was two 70-kg (154-pound) bombs. The hangar was 22 meters long and could hold all three aircraft.

HANDLING

The ship was a good "sea boat." She rode well and moved gently but responded slowly to the helm. The turning radius was 450 meters.

COST

The *Prinz Eugen* cost 104.5 million RM ($42 million U.S.). To put this in perspective, *Bismarck* cost 196.8 million RM, the light cruiser *Nürnberg* 40 million RM, a type VII C submarine 4.7 million RM. In 1940 2.5 RM = $1.00 U.S. This compares unfavorably to the cost of a U.S. *New Orleans*–class cruiser, approximately $12 million. Not until the *Baltimore*-class did the cost of U.S. heavy cruisers reach $40 million per hull.

Other *Prince Eugenes*

Prominent warships named after Prince Eugene include HMS *Prince Eugene* (a British monitor), the Italian light cruiser *Eugenio di Savoia*, and the Austro-Hungarian central-battery ship and battleship *Prinz Eugen*. It is hard to think of another man who had major warships from four different nations named after him.

HMS *Prince Eugene* was a *Lord Clive*–class monitor. The ships in this class were named after famous generals, and Prince Eugene had been a British ally during the War of the Spanish Succession (1701–14), when he fought alongside John Churchill, the Duke of Marlborough. This vessel displaced 6,150 tons, was 335 feet long, could steam at 6.5 knots, and was armed with a pair of breech-loading 12-inch rifles in a single turret and two 3-inch guns. She

Austro-Hungarian broadside ironclad *Prinz Eugen*. She was reconstructed as a central-battery ship and finally ended her career as an active warship in 1904, before being claimed by Italy in 1919 as a war prize. (NHHC)

Austro-Hungarian dreadnought *Prinz Eugen*. (NHHC)

served in the English Channel and off the Belgian coast from late 1915 supporting destroyers and mine-warfare vessels and bombarding coastal targets. She fought at Zeebrugge, where her target (ironically) was the Tirpitz Battery, and at Ostend in April and May 1918.

The first Austro-Hungarian *Prinz Eugen*, a broadside ironclad, was launched in 1862 and rebuilt in 1877. In her final configuration she displaced 3,548 tons. The second *Prinz Eugen* was laid down in 1912 and completed just in time for war on 17 July 1914. She displaced 20,000 tons, was 499 feet long overall, had a speed of 20 knots, and was armed with twelve 305-mm/45, twelve 15-cm/50 and eighteen 66-mm/50 guns, and four 533-mm torpedoes. The Austro-Hungarian dreadnoughts were major national assets but had little purpose in the Adriatic naval war fought against Italy and the allied powers between 1915 and 1918. She participated only in the 9 June 1918 sortie of the fleet that led to the sinking of her sister *Szent István* by an Italian motor torpedo boat. After the war *Prinz Eugen* was handed over to France and was expended as a target ship in 1922.

The Italian cruiser *Eugenio di Savoia* had the most active career of all the ships named after Prince Eugene of Savoy. She was laid down in 1933 and commissioned in January 1936. She displaced 8,450 tons, had a length of 613 feet, a practical speed of 32 knots, and was armed with eight 152-mm/53, six 100-mm/47, and eight 37-mm guns and six 533-mm torpedoes. She laid mines or protected minelaying forces on several occasions in June 1940 and May–June 1941; she participated in the Battle of Calabria in July 1940; bombarded Greek positions in December 1940; covered convoys to Africa in April and May 1941 and February, March, and April 1942; disabled the British destroyer *Bedouin* during the Battle of Pantelleria in June 1942; and sortied against the U.S. Navy in August 1943. After the war she was handed to the Greeks and finally ended her active career in 1965.

PRINZ EUGEN READIES FOR WAR, AND GERMANY'S NAVAL STRATEGY

Prinz Eugen at Kiel on 1 August 1940. (NHHC)

Prinz Eugen commissioned on 1 August 1940, eleven months into the war. Admiral Raeder sent a message to the ship on this occasion: "Acknowledge with thanks report concerning commissioning of cruiser *Prinz Eugen*. I expect that her action readiness will be speedily established, so that the crew may have an early opportunity of doing honor to her glorious name. I wish the Commander and the crew of *Prinz Eugen* godspeed and all success." The ship's first captain, Helmuth Brinkmann, addressed the crew on the occasion and reportedly said, "We are a happy ship and we are a lucky ship. . . . But in the long run luck comes only to those who deserve it!"

At this point in the war the German navy was adjusting to the losses and damage it had suffered in the Norwegian campaign. *Prinz Eugen*'s sister ship, *Blücher*, had been sunk by enemy shore batteries. *Admiral Hipper*, which had returned to Germany on 11 August after an unproductive raiding cruise in Arctic waters, spent the rest of the month in dock to have her troublesome engines attended to. The possibility of invading England loomed large in navy planning. The army's desire for a landing on a broad front was particularly worrisome, because the larger warships needed to protect and support such an operation were not available. The new battleships *Bismarck* and

Tirpitz were months away from being operational. The undergunned battleships *Gneisenau* and *Scharnhorst* had just finished a sortie into the Norwegian Sea that had resulted in the sinking of the British aircraft carrier *Glorious*. *Gneisenau* had been torpedoed by a British submarine and would be in dock through 21 October 1940, while *Scharnhorst* needed repairs that would take through 21 November. Thus, any near-term invasion of England would have to be undertaken without a major German naval presence.

Prinz Eugen's first captain was *Kapitän zur See* Helmuth Brinkmann, a World War I veteran who had served in battleships, cruisers, and destroyers. He had entered the navy in 1913 as a Sea Cadet and earned promotion to *Leutnant zur See* in September 1915. During the war he first served on the predreadnought battleships *Kaiser Friedrich III* and *Kaiser Karl der Grosse*. From March through October 1915 he was radio officer of the light cruiser *Regensburg* and after that served in a succession of torpedo boats, *G196*, *G192*, *V190*, and *S133*. He participated in at least one surface action, in which British light cruisers of the Harwich Force supporting a seaplane raid against a German airbase south of Denmark clashed with German units, including *G196*. He remained in the navy after the war, earning promotion to *Kapitanleutnant* in 1925, *Korvettenkapitän*

***Prinz Eugen* at Kiel on 1 August 1940. She is being assisted by a tug. The man on the stern is using a megaphone to communicate with the dock, probably about casting off the line. (U.S. Naval Institute photo archive)**

Crew loading ammunition. (U.S. Naval Institute photo archive)

and August 1940 Brinkmann served in various staff positions for the German admiralty.

On 2 July 1940 still fitting out at Kiel, the new cruiser experienced an air raid by five Whitleys armed with twenty-four 250-pound and sixteen 500-pound bombs and by eleven Hampdens with one 1000-pound and forty 500-pound bombs. *Scharnhorst*, which had just entered dock was the main target. The battleship was not hit, but *Prinz Eugen* took a 500-pound bomb on the port side and suffered some minor structural damage. This did not seriously delay her commissioning. The attackers claimed to have scored several direct hits and near misses and to have started a fire that could be seen thirty-five miles away. The Admiralty war diary noted after the attack that "photographs reveal that damage was not so extensive as would appear from the above reports."

in January 1933, *Fregattenkapitän* in January 1937 and finally *Kapitän zur See* in October 1938. His last billet before taking over *Prinz Eugen* was as commanding officer of the state yacht *Grille*. Between May 1938

German Naval Strategy and Policy up through May 1941

EXCERPT FROM "UNPREPARED BUT UNDAUNTED" BY PETER HOOKER, *NAVAL HISTORY*, DECEMBER 2017

The German Navy, or Kriegsmarine, played a key role during World War II by attempting to sever Britain's sea lines of communication, providing support during littoral land operations, and taking the conflict at sea as far as the U.S. East Coast and the Indian and Pacific oceans. While the Kriegsmarine's historical narrative overwhelmingly is dominated by the U-boat campaign, German surface warships made an invaluable contribution to the war effort that provides an astute demonstration of how a small, albeit well-equipped, navy can exercise a remarkable degree of naval power against a vastly superior opponent.

The Offensive's Slow Start

At the outbreak of war in September 1939, the German surface fleet

Grand Admiral Erich Raeder. In World War I he served as Admiral Hipper's chief of staff and participated in the battles of Dogger Bank and Jutland. He led the German navy from 1928 to January 1943 and was a proponent of a large, balanced fleet. (U.S. Naval Institute photo archive)

consisted of seven capital ships: two obsolete predreadnought battleships, two battle cruisers, and three heavily armed cruisers, or *Panzerschiffe* (armored ships), that were nicknamed "pocket battleships." In comparison, the Royal Navy could deploy 15 capital ships and 7 aircraft carriers. Despite the overwhelming odds, Kriegsmarine Commander-in-Chief Admiral Erich Raeder knew from his experience in World War I that his capital ships would likely degrade into an ineffective force if left in port as a fleet-in-being. He therefore ordered plans to be drawn up for an immediate offensive against Britain's sea lines of communication.

Before the war, Raeder had hoped to construct a fleet of 10 capital ships, 8 aircraft carriers, and 12 updated pocket battleships, along with some

249 U-boats—the Z-Plan Fleet. The strategic thought underlying the Z-Plan was that the fleet would be split into two forces: a North Sea defensive force and an Atlantic offensive force. The latter was to be divided into a series of small, asymmetrical task forces charged with attacking the enemy's sea lines. A supply system of disguised merchant ships was to keep the task forces at optimum efficiency.

With the Z-Plan nowhere near complete by 1939, Raeder instead hoped to throw all his available units at the British in the hope of disrupting enough merchant shipping and naval operations to provide time for the build-up of a strong U-boat force that could implement an economic blockade and practice sea denial.

Raeder faced considerable political and operational obstacles in executing this strategy. Believing he could negotiate peace with Britain, Adolf Hitler delayed orders for the Kriegsmarine to commence operations against British forces. When the order finally came, the pocket battleship *Deutschland* was ordered back to Germany and out of danger. Raeder reasoned that the sinking of a ship bearing such an illustrious name would be a severe blow to the morale of the German people. This left only the pocket battleship *Graf Spee* deployed outside the North Sea. Her crew eventually scuttled her on 17 December 1939, after the Battle of the River Plate in which she damaged three Royal Navy cruisers but was severely damaged herself. Not only was Raeder now deprived of two units in the Atlantic, but the scuttling also brought the Kriegsmarine under the German high command's scrutiny.

The April 1940 German invasion of Norway required all available naval units for transporting and supporting troops. The operation, although ultimately a success, resulted in the loss of the heavy cruiser *Blücher*, as well as 12 destroyers. The battle cruisers *Scharnhorst* and *Gneisenau* were damaged, as was the *Lützow* (the newly renamed *Deutschland*) and the heavy cruiser *Admiral Hipper*. Nonetheless, the Germans sank five British destroyers and damaged the battle cruiser *Renown*, during the first engagement of the war between capital ships.

Heavy cruiser *Admiral Hipper* and a Type IX/A submarine pictured in an icy German port. (U.S. Naval Institute photo archive)

The conquest of Norway had significant strategic consequences. It forced the British Home Fleet to conduct its operations farther west in the Denmark Strait, between Greenland and Iceland, where there was less risk from German air attack, and with the seizure of French coastal ports, Raeder now had a significant geographical advantage over the British. His forces could run the gauntlet of the Denmark Strait and dock in a French coastal port, from where they could easily renew attacks on enemy sea lines of communication.

The German Navy also had regained faith with Hitler, who now allowed Raeder to pursue his strategy. The significant losses to the surface fleet, however, meant that the price was high, and the fleet never fully recovered.

In October 1940, the *Admiral Scheer* became the first German capital ship to break out into the Atlantic during wartime. Showcasing the qualities of the pocket battleships, as well as the efficiency of the supply system in a voyage stretching as far as the Indian Ocean, the *Scheer* sank 99,059 tons before returning to Germany in March 1941. Her attack on Convoy HX 84 in the North Atlantic resulted in the sinking of five ships totaling 38,720 tons, along with the escorting armed merchant cruiser *Jervis Bay*. Though a relatively minor achievement, the attack caused the next two HX (eastbound) convoys to be recalled to port and held up further convoys for 12 days. The *Admiral Hipper* made a follow-up sortie in November and achieved meager results, but she was the first heavy German warship to successfully put into the French port of Brest, in December 1940, where she posed a more immediate threat to Atlantic shipping.

Meanwhile, disguised auxiliary cruisers were deployed into the Atlantic, Indian, and Pacific oceans. In July, one auxiliary cruiser would force the Admiralty to stop all independent shipping and divert convoys away from the West Indies, while another, the *Atlantis*, would sink a record 145,687 tons before meeting her end in November 1941 against the heavy cruiser HMS *Devonshire*.

As expected, these operations dispersed British naval power and moved focus away from U-boats. The Royal Navy dispatched three task forces, including four cruisers and two aircraft carriers, to find the *Scheer*. A sighting by the light cruiser HMS *Glasgow* brought an additional carrier and four cruisers into the hunt.

On 25 December 1940, the *Hipper* intercepted a convoy carrying 40,000 troops to the Middle East but was driven off after a brief engagement with British escorts. This encounter nonetheless had significant consequences, as the Admiralty rushed to assign heavy warships to escort convoys. Though fewer antisubmarine warfare–equipped vessels were diverted than was expected by the German Naval High Command, the commitment of heavy escorts underlined the Admiralty's anxiety and the threat posed by Raeder's surface fleet. The worst, however, was yet to come.

The Peak Period

In January 1941, the *Scharnhorst* and *Gneisenau*, under the command of Vice Admiral Günther Lütjens, ventured into the Atlantic. During the operation, code-named Berlin, the two battle cruisers, aided by nine supply ships, sank or captured 116,610 tons of shipping over 60 days. It was the largest and most successful Atlantic operation by the German surface fleet during the war. Distant cooperation between the *Scharnhorst*, *Gneisenau*, and U-boats led to the tracking and interception of Convoy SL 67 on 7–8 March that resulted in the submarines sinking five ships.

GERMAN SURFACE ACTIONS 1940–41

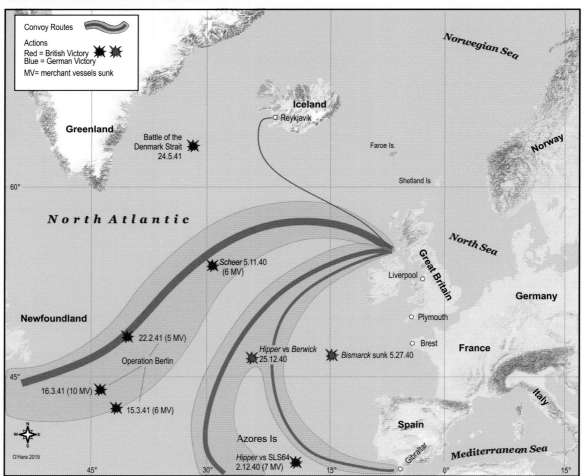

(Created by the Author)

Before steering for France, Lütjens intercepted several more merchant ships that had been dispersed from a convoy because of a U-boat attack.

On 9–11 February, during the *Hipper*'s second Atlantic sortie, *U-37*, Fw-200 Condor reconnaissance bombers, and the heavy cruiser carried out the first successful asymmetrical operation in history against Convoy HG 30. This also led to the *Hipper*'s greatest success, when on the next day she sank 7 of 19 unescorted ships of Convoy SLS 64.

Dispersed as it was, the British fleet could not deal effectively with the multifaceted threat. Official historian of the Royal Navy Stephen Roskill noted that during this period surface ships caused the loss of much shipping and, "for a time, completely dislocated our Atlantic convoy circles, with serious consequences to our vital imports. Their [the *Scharnhorst*'s and *Gneisenau*'s] depredations forced the wide dispersal of our already strained naval resources, and successfully diverted attention from the returning *Scheer* and *Hipper*; while, by

their subsequent arrival in a Biscay port, they became an imminent threat to all our Atlantic shipping."

January to March 1941 thus marks the offensive peak of the German surface fleet. No less than four heavy warships were active, and the period also marks the first successful combined sea operations. The activities of the surface fleet were particularly significant as the number of operational U-boats reached a wartime low. As such, it was left to the warships and auxiliary cruisers to keep pressure on Britain.

The German navy did not rush its new ships into action even in the face of such major needs as an impending invasion of England. Upon commissioning, *Prinz Eugen* started working up. On 22 August, after taking on stores and practice ammunition and being inspected by the Admiral Cruisers, she left Kiel for Gotenhafen. On 27 August the new cruiser conducted fuel-consumption and speed trials. Throughout September she tested her equipment, hydrophones, and radars and practiced underway replenishment. Gunnery exercises started in October, and on the 15th of that month she fired her big guns for the first time. Battle training started in November, but this was interrupted by a spell in dock that lasted from 3 November through 13 December to fix defects and wrap up incomplete work. Live ammunition was loaded and more speed trials run, showing a speed of 33.5 knots. Intensive battle training followed and then, from 25 January through 8 April, more time in dock, during which workers completed modifications found necessary during the working-up period.

By April 1941 *Grossadmiral* Raeder's strategy of using heavy ships for cruiser warfare was proving successful. *Scheer* and *Hipper* had just returned from North Atlantic forays where they sank twenty-five freighters totaling 144,275 GRT; German raiders were active on Allied sea-lanes in three oceans; and *Gneisenau* and *Scharnhorst* were safe in Brest after a two-month rampage through

Preparing to leave Kiel, early 1941. Note bedspring radar antennas mounted on the front of *Prinz Eugen*'s range-finder shields. Also note folding propeller guard attached to the side of her hull. (NHHC)

Admiral Lütjens inspecting *Prinz Eugen*'s crew after the ship was assigned to his command for Operation *Rheinübung*. (U.S. Naval Institute photo archive)

the North Atlantic. They had sunk 116,610 GRT of shipping, despite restrictive rules of engagement and cautious handling, and completely disrupted the British convoy system. *Bismarck* and *Prinz Eugen* were nearly ready for action. Raeder was putting the final touches on an operation that would deliver the mightiest strike yet against Britain's beleaguered Atlantic supply line: simultaneous sorties by the three battleships and *Prinz Eugen*.

Prinz Eugen sailed from Deutsche Werke on 8 April 1941 to Gotenhafen. Here, in preparation for her first war assignment she conducted an extensive exercise program. In speed trials conducted at 75 percent load she achieved 32.84 knots. After exercising with *Bismarck* on the 22nd she set sail for Kiel, escorted by the mine breaker *Rothenburg*. On the 23rd there was an underwater explosion in the wake of the escort, roughly 25 meters off the cruiser's starboard bow. The explosion shook the ship and caused a loss of power and steam. In less than an hour, however, *Prinz Eugen* was again under way; she docked at Kiel to assess the damage. This proved to consist of ruptured fuel bunkers, damaged propeller shafts, a generator knocked from its foundation, and shock damage to delicate systems like fire control and electricity. Corrections required a week in dock. She did not get

under way to Gotenhafen for final preparations until 11 May.

Operation *Rheinübung* as originally planned would have severely stressed Great Britain's North Atlantic convoy system, but it was also a great risk. Once *Rheinübung* was reduced to just *Bismarck* and *Prinz Eugen*, the odds were much less favorable for the Germans. With the advent of spring the hours of darkness were getting shorter, but the most critical weakness in the operation as it developed was the fact that both ships, although in commission nine months, were still not completely worked up. They were new ships with raw crews, and sending them out together on such a difficult mission was a daring roll of the dice.

Grand Admiral Raeder's philosophy regarding the use of his major surface assets was explained in a directive issued on 23 May 1940. It criticized the cautious orthodoxy he had found among his operational commands and urged a "new offensive spirit," particularly in the use of battleships. "I am ultimately convinced," he wrote, "that the loss of one of these [battleships] would little change the situation at sea or the war's final outcome, but through continuous action much can be won. By not using them, or by delaying their use, we not only gain nothing, we lose the future of the Navy as well."

Bismarck: Not Ready for Action?

EXCERPT FROM "BISMARCK: NOT READY FOR ACTION?" BY TIMOTHY P. MULLIGAN, *NAVAL HISTORY*, FEBRUARY 2001

[Raeder's] guideline [regarding a new offensive spirit] remained in force as the *Bismarck* prepared for operations. Impressive as she was, the *Bismarck* remained a new ship with a new crew about to enter combat for the first time. The commander, *Kapitän zur See* Ernst Lindemann, together with his first officer, first artillery officer, and engineering officer, all were highly capable and qualified men who had served in instructional schools or in staff positions—but none had seen action since the war began. As his ship was rushed through final preparations before departing on operations, Lindemann offered a modest yet intriguing assessment of the *Bismarck's* status in the war diary on 28 April 1941:

"The training level attained compares well with that for a capital ship in the prewar years. If the crew for the most part lacks actual combat experience, I am nevertheless confident that this ship could fulfill any mission demanded of it. This feeling is strengthened by the vessel's material combat quality, which in combination with the attained training level has produced such a level of confidence in everyone that, for the first time in a long while, we feel ourselves at least the equal of any opponent."

Lindemann's caution doubtless reflected a concern over the loss of invaluable training and sea trials time to the severe winter of 1941. After her commissioning on 20 August 1940, the *Bismarck* accomplished some basic training and tests in the Baltic from September to early December 1940, then returned to her home port

of Hamburg. With that harbor and the Kaiser Wilhelm Canal (now the Kiel Canal) iced over throughout the winter, the *Bismarck* had to postpone the resumption of Baltic training from late January to early March. The severity of the cold, with temperatures falling to -15° C (about 5° F), froze up pressure gauges and electrical lines and forced a temporary shutdown of the boiler rooms. By the time the battleship could transfer to the Baltic, five irreplaceable weeks of at-sea training had been lost.

Perhaps even more important, the intensified training that followed could not build on the experiences gained during the two-month commerce raiding sortie (codenamed Operation Berlin) just completed by the battlecruisers *Scharnhorst* and *Gneisenau*. Their experiences during the North Atlantic winter already had led to one modification on board the *Bismarck*—the removal of the 10.5-m stereoscopic rangefinder from the forward main battery Turret "Anton," because it was overly prone to water damage from running seas. When the two older vessels, which already had seen extensive action in the North Sea and off Norway, finally put into Brest on 22 March 1941, the *Bismarck* had commenced her final exercises in the Gulf of Danzig. On board the *Scharnhorst* and *Gneisenau*, division officers prepared detailed reports of lessons learned during Operation Berlin in the areas of navigation, communications, ordnance, signaling, and medical considerations, while specialists detailed the performance of radio, radar, and encryption equipment.

These reports naturally required study and comment by several staffs before the final recommendations were approved and acted upon, procedures that demanded patience and time. The rush to commit the *Bismarck* to action, however, negated the benefits of this evaluation process. Lindemann was hard pressed to apply only the most practical lessons of the operation, which proved difficult enough—refueling at sea, the launching and recovery of onboard aircraft, gunnery and damage control drills, cooperation with U-boats, and joint movements in formation.

All but ignored in the rush were the even more critical lessons at the command level. Admiral Lütjens had directed Operation Berlin by a precarious juggling of his own judgment as fleet commander against the instructions of the Seekriegsleitung (Naval War Staff), the operational guidance of Naval Group Commands North and West (depending on the vessels' location), and on occasion the instincts of his battlecruisers' captains. Although the 22 Allied merchant ships sunk or captured marked the operation a success, many differences of opinion had emerged over specific actions taken and prospective opportunities won or lost. Lütjens himself had no time to reflect on these matters, as preparations for the upcoming *Rheinübung* (Exercise Rhine) kept him shuttling constantly among Brest, Berlin, Paris, Kiel, and Swinemünde. These vital command issues remained unexamined and unresolved, and played a significant role in the *Bismarck's* ill-fated sortie.

Ironically, the question of the *Bismarck*'s readiness for action already had cast a shadow on the history of Operation Berlin. Hardly had the *Scharnhorst* and *Gneisenau* broken into the Atlantic when, on 8 February 1941, the Seekriegsleitung directed Group Command North to prepare for joint exercises of the *Bismarck* and *Prinz Eugen*. This first reference to the latter warships acting together obviously anticipated the next stage in surface operations, yet it came at a time when the *Bismarck* was still frozen in Hamburg harbor. On 12 March—while the *Bismarck* stood in Kiel harbor, about to begin her final workup exercises—Admiral Lütjens received instructions to curtail Operation Berlin so as to have the *Scharnhorst* and *Gneisenau* available to renew operations at the end of April, in combination with the planned breakout of the *Bismarck* and *Prinz Eugen*. This effectively ended Berlin, as both of the former ships needed refitting and repairs, and only the *Gneisenau* possibly could meet an April deadline to renew operations (in the end she too fell out because of damage sustained in air attacks while in Brest). Thus, the most successful fleet commerce raid ended in part to accommodate a fixed timetable of the *Bismarck*'s presumed availability, despite the lengthy delays already imposed on her readiness by severe weather.

Lindemann learned only on 19 March that his ship was expected to be ready for operations by the end of April. The Seekriegsleitung's need to maintain secrecy not only kept the battleship's commanding officer in the dark about the planned timetable, but thereby further reduced his training time. To complete preparations and final outfitting for operations, Lindemann had to plan on completing all training and ordnance tests by 2 April, eliminating an additional three to four weeks of exercises from his already foreshortened training program. And even that limited time suffered inroads from the need to address nagging material problems, particularly the operation of the side cranes (described by Lindemann as "extremely delicate and unreliable") and continual replacement of glass panes and slide valves broken or dislodged by practice firings of the main guns.

Ultimately, the fixed timetable that had so determined the tempo of events itself fell victim to developments beyond its control. As of 2 April plans still called for the *Gneisenau*'s eventual participation in the operation, but severe damage by British air attacks on 6 and 10 April would immobilize her for at least four months at Brest. Rheinübung remained on schedule to begin on 28 April, but with only five days to go the *Prinz Eugen* struck a mine outside Kiel. The explosion damaged fuel bunkers, propeller shafts, and a turbo-generator, forcing the cruiser into dry-dock for nine days and finally revising the timetable so rigidly adhered to up to this point. In a meeting with Raeder on 26 April, Lütjens raised the possibility of postponing the operation until the *Scharnhorst* or even the *Tirpitz* could participate as well, but the original plan remained in place and they awaited the completion of the *Prinz Eugen*'s repairs. In the end, the cruiser required more work than originally planned, and a recurrence of the *Bismarck*'s chronic problem with the port crane on 14 May imposed a further delay. Rheinübung finally began on 18 May, nearly three weeks behind schedule.

In some respects, the German navy was walking a tightrope. It had insufficient assets for the tasks it wanted to accomplish. It needed to deploy its resources regardless of whether they were ready, or even appropriate for the task. It had to follow a policy of caution, because not a single major vessel of the navy could be considered expendable. The Norwegian campaign had shown what the navy could accomplish if it acted without restraint, but the loss of *Blücher*, two light cruisers, and twelve destroyers also showed the consequences of unrestrained use. Operation Berlin seemed to promise a template whereby the surface fleet could exercise a real influence on the war, and Raeder should be credited for trying to establish an environment wherein such operations became routine. However, as *Prinz Eugen*'s subsequent career would show, the British Royal Navy was a skilled opponent, and the margins within which the German navy had to practice the type of naval warfare it wanted to practice were narrow indeed.

OPERATION *RHEINÜBUNG*

WITH *BISMARCK* AND ALONE IN THE NORTH ATLANTIC, MAY 1942

EXCERPT FROM *GERMAN FLEET AT WAR, 1939–45* BY VINCENT P. O'HARA

Operation *Rheinübung* finally commenced on 18 May, three weeks behind schedule, with only *Bismarck* and *Prinz Eugen* participating. It was commanded by Admiral Günther Lütjens, flying his flag on *Bismarck*. Lütjens wasn't even out of the Baltic, however, before the British had news of his sailing. Surprise was critical to *Rheinübung*'s success, but Lütjens regained some advantage when he slipped away from Bergen, Norway, unseen on the evening of the 21st. There were only three exits into the broad reaches of the North Atlantic; against the advice of Naval Group North Lütjens elected the most distant and narrowest, the Denmark Strait. It had served him well several months before.

Bismarck at sea en route to Norway, circa 19–20 May 1941, prior to her Atlantic sortie. Photographed from *Prinz Eugen*. (NHHC)

Bismarck in a Norwegian fjord, 21 May 1941, shortly before departing for her Atlantic sortie. Photographed from *Prinz Eugen*. Location is probably Grimstadfjord, just south of Bergen. *Bismarck*'s camouflage was painted over before she departed the area. (NHHC)

The next day in Scapa Flow Admiral John C. Tovey, commander of the Home Fleet flying his flag on board *King George V*, learned *Bismarck* had vanished from Norwegian waters. He had already sent Vice Admiral Lancelot Holland's Battle Cruiser Squadron consisting of *Hood*, *Prince of Wales* (Captain J. C. Leach), and six destroyers toward Iceland. He deployed his other forces based upon the enemy's possible routes, the most likely of which he considered to be the Denmark Strait. He then led *King George V*, the aircraft carrier *Victorious*, four cruisers, and seven destroyers to sea to await events.

In May the Greenland ice pack limited navigation in the Denmark Strait, the body of water between Greenland and Iceland, to a channel about seventy miles wide. British minefields running northwest from Vestfirdir in Iceland further constricted the passage to just ten miles. The heavy cruisers of the 1st Cruiser Squadron, *Norfolk*, flagship of Rear Admiral F. Wake-Walker and *Suffolk*, guarded this bottleneck. *Suffolk* had a newly installed Type 279 radar that projected visibility up to thirteen miles forward, although it was blind aft. The cruisers had been on their unpopular and uneventful patrol for days. On the afternoon of 23

HMS *Hood*, the largest warship in the world during the 1920s and 1930s. She represented British naval might, and her destruction by *Bismarck* and *Prinz Eugen* was a profound shock to the British nation. (Watercolor by Edward Tufnell, RN [Ret.], NHHC)

UNITED STATES NAVAL INSTITUTE

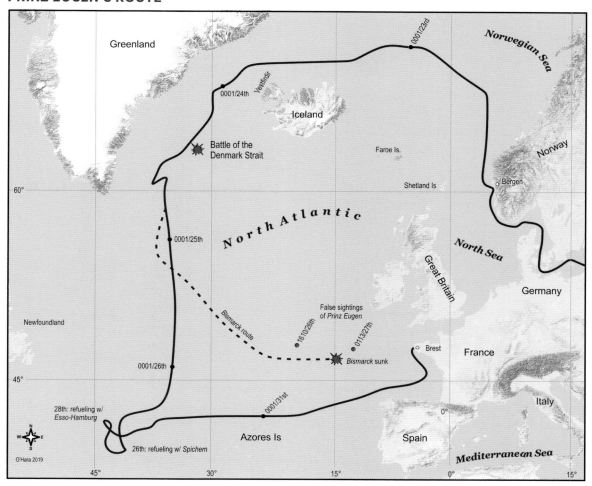

(Created by the Author)

May the weather was uncommonly fine with scattered snow flurries, clear water along the ice edge and good visibility over Greenland, although fog blanketed the Icelandic side of the passage. The sea, capable of such violence, was relatively benign.

Based on faulty aerial reconnaissance of Scapa Flow, Lütjens believed the British Home Fleet was in harbor; he was cautiously confident that surprise was his and the operation was successfully on course. *Bismarck*, leading *Prinz Eugen* and hugging the edge of the pack ice, approached the Vestfirdir narrows on the evening of the 23rd. At 1922 hours, shortly after she had turned to the southwest after completing the northern leg of her patrol, *Suffolk* sighted two ships on her same course about seven miles north. She turned to port and slipped into the mist at the edge of the minefields. German hydrophones and radar likewise detected *Suffolk*, but Lütjens continued on course. He expected cruisers to be patrolling the exits into the North Atlantic, but he

might have acted differently had he known Holland was only 250 miles away steering a converging course while Tovey was six hundred miles to the southeast.

Norfolk, operating fifteen miles abeam of *Suffolk*, hurried north to close the contact. At 2030 she accidentally emerged from the fog bank only six miles south of *Bismarck*. *Bismarck* fired five 38-cm salvos and straddled the cruiser throwing splinters aboard. *Norfolk* came hard about and regained the safety of the fog. The blast from her heavy guns disabled *Bismarck*'s forward radar set. For this reason, and because he wanted *Bismarck*'s guns to cover the cruisers which were now trailing astern, Lütjens ordered *Prinz Eugen* to take the lead. The Germans steamed south at 30 knots, followed by the British ten to fourteen miles behind.

At 0012 on the 24th Vice Admiral Holland, leading the *Hood*, *Prince of Wales*, and four destroyers altered course from northwest to north-northwest. He hoped to cross in front of the enemy in two hours, just after

Bismarck following *Prinz Eugen*. This photo shows them exercising underway replenishment just before the operation. (NHHC)

sunset. This would silhouette the German ships against the setting sun, giving him the advantage of light. Moreover, by crossing the enemy's T his full broadside would bear while the Germans would be limited to their forward turrets. However, shortly before his change of course, *Suffolk* lost contact with *Bismarck* in a snowstorm. When he received this news, Holland could no longer predict the point of interception. At 0017 he altered to due north and reduced speed to 25 knots. Still hoping to obtain surprise, he maintained radio silence.

By luck or instinct, Holland's new course would have resulted in the interception he desired. At 0140 his destroyers passed only ten miles southeast of *Bismarck*, which had altered course a little to the west keeping to the edge of the pack ice. But at this time the visibility was three miles and the forces passed unseen. At 0205 Holland turned back to the south-southwest fearing the Germans had altered course to the southeast and that *Bismarck* might pass astern, although he instructed his destroyers to continue searching to the north. As Stephen Roskill, the British official historian, wrote: "Holland's guess was wrong[;] . . . [his] action had the unhappy result of causing his squadron to lose bearing on the enemy—or, less technically expressed, to drop behind."

At 0247 *Suffolk* regained contact. *Bismarck* had never deviated substantially from her original course; Holland had lost his lead and his destroyers were scattered. For the next three hours the British admiral maneuvered to undo the damage. At 0321 he came to course 220° and at 0342 to 240°, speed 28 knots. By 0400 *Bismarck* was only twenty miles northwest of *Hood* on a parallel, slightly converging course. Visibility had improved to twelve miles. At 0440 Holland further modified course 40° to starboard in order to close range. His destroyers trailed thirty miles behind. Although he intended to have the cruisers engage *Prinz Eugen* while he fought *Bismarck*, he never told Wake-Walker he was approaching, and they were too far north to intervene when he appeared.

All of Holland's efforts and sacrifices to achieve surprise, however, were meaningless. *Prinz Eugen*'s hydrophones had caught the sounds of the British heavy units long before. At 0535 when *Prince of Wales* established visual contact the two forces were about 29,000 yards apart, steering on slightly converging courses, the British on 240° and the Germans on 220°.

Bismarck, *Prinz Eugen*, and *Prince of Wales* were all facing action for the first time. *Bismarck* and *Prinz Eugen*—completed in August 1940—were worked up while the builders had delivered *Prince of Wales* a scant seven weeks before, hardly time to correct mechanical problems much less train a battleship's crew. She even had a hundred Vickers-Armstrong workers fixing last-minute defects. *Hood*, a more experienced ship, was old, unmodernized, and had an inadequate fire-control system. She was particularly vulnerable to long-range shell fire.

Weather and visibility had improved, although the northern twilight was not due to end for another hour. Holland altered course at 0537 turning 40° toward the Germans. Lütjens responded two minutes later, turning 45° away from the British, coming to course 265°. This alteration decreased the rate of closing and caused the rear turrets of the British ships to lose bearing. Holland maintained his heading until 0549. With the range at nearly 26,000 yards he altered 20° to starboard to course 300°. This resulted in an angle of convergence of 35° and a closing rate of 520 yards per minute. *Prince of Wales* followed the flag 2,400 yards off her starboard quarter. Holland knew well *Hood's* vulnerability to long-range fire, and it seems to have been his intention to close as rapidly as possible. However, he had "in effect allowed the enemy to cross his T by his own course alterations." Lütjens was still uncertain what he was facing, but the enemy's speed told him that they were not old battleships he could outmaneuver.

The battle began at 0552 when *Hood* opened fire at *Prinz Eugen* from 25,000 yards. Her shots fell as close as 100 yards ahead and 50 yards to port of the cruiser. The next salvo saw one shell land 50 yards ahead, sending some splinters on board. The fourth salvo dropped squarely in the cruiser's wake. *Hood* was getting the range, but she was firing on the wrong ship. Despite orders to target the lead ship, *Prince of Wales* shot at *Bismarck* from the beginning and after four salvos, *Hood* finally switched targets herself. By now, Lütjens knew he was facing fast battleships. At 0553/54 he ordered his column to bend 65° to port to course 200° in order to open his arcs of fire.

The British had fired four or five times before *Bismarck* and *Prinz Eugen* settled on their new course and replied at 0555, both targeting *Hood*. The range from *Bismarck* was approximately 21,500 yards and from *Prinz Eugen* 22,000 yards. At the same time Holland responded to the German maneuver—and to the fact Lütjens was crossing his T—by ordering a turn 20° to port, back to 280°.

According to the report he filed, *Prinz Eugen's* gunnery officer, Commander Paulus Jasper, did not appreciate that the enemy ships were battleships and thus employed HE base-fuzed shells. "I persisted in using this type of projectile during the course of the battle, since their impacts differentiated them very well from other [impacts]." When at 0555 he received permission he fired a full eight-gun broadside from 20,200 meters. He could not spot the first salvo, because the ready ammunition was nose-fuzed and could not be distinguished from other splashes. The second broadside, also of eight guns, allowed Jasper to determine that two rounds were short and the others over. From the third salvo he saw "an extraordinarily bright fire flash appear on the enemy

ship's aft section at the level of the aft mast." *Prinz Eugen* had struck the battle's first blow and started a massive fire aft in *Hood's* ready-use ammunition on the boat deck, near one of her twin 4-inch antiaircraft mountings. Immediately thereafter *Prinz Eugen* was ordered to shift fire to *Prince of Wales* on the principle that no enemy should be permitted to fire unengaged. *Bismarck* obtained straddles against *Hood* with her second and third salvos; the fourth fell short but very close.

Initially German shooting outmatched that of the British. Up to 0600 *Prince of Wales* fired nine times, but turret problems—the bane of her class—limited these to five-, and then three-gun salvos (of the six guns in her two forward turrets). She straddled with her

Prince of Wales (left smoke column) turns to open the range, after she was hit by German gunfire. Smoke at right marks the spot where HMS *Hood* had exploded and sunk a few minutes earlier. (NHHC)

sixth, but the fine angle and high speed of the approach prevented the British from obtaining accurate ranges. Moreover, the Germans enjoyed the weather gage, and sea and spray affected the British forward range finders. The 42-foot range finder in the battleship's A turret was largely underwater. Another disadvantage suffered by the British was their diagonal angle of approach, which increased the probability of shells from a German spread striking them, while the German parallel angle decreased the likelihood of a British hit.

Against *Prince of Wales*, *Prinz Eugen* fired a full broadside at 0558 and then a ranging group that acquired the target. She then began firing for effect, the range being 16,000–17,000 meters. She aimed eight salvoes at the British battleship up through 0601 and eventually scored four hits. Although *Prince of Wales* came within extreme torpedo range, *Prinz Eugen* did not launch torpedoes. Her torpedo officer considered the odds of hitting too low. German naval staff would criticize him for this after the battle.

The decisive moment of the battle came at 0600. Holland had just ordered a 20-degree turn to port so all eight guns would bear when *Bismarck*'s fifth salvo arrived. The range was 17,000 yards. One or more shells struck *Hood* near her mainmast. Captain Leech recalled, "There was a very fierce upward rush of flame the shape of a funnel . . . and almost instantaneously the ship was enveloped in smoke from one end to the other." A tremendous explosion followed. One of her crew saw "the whole forward section of *Hood* rear up from the water like the spire of a cathedral, towering above the upper deck of *Prince of Wales* as she steamed by." *Prince of Wales* turned hard to starboard to avoid the wreckage, thereby also closing the enemy so that even *Prinz Eugen*'s 10.5-cm guns opened fire. The German cruiser's second gunnery officer wrote, "After *Hood*'s explosion and loss of forward motion, [*Prince of Wales*] steamed between it and the German ships. Her appearance was very blurred by thick smoke so that, as was the case with *Hood*, only shells falling short or direct hits could be observed. Muzzle flashes and flashes from detonating shells were difficult to differentiate."

By 0602 *Prince of Wales* had returned to course 260 and resumed fire. The distance between her and *Bismarck* was down to 15,500 yards. With *Hood* gone, it took *Bismarck* just a minute to shift fire and find the range. At 0602 a 38-cm shell passed through *Prince of Wales*' bridge without exploding, although splinters killed or wounded everyone present except Captain Leach and one other man. At 0603 *Bismarck* began passing *Prinz Eugen*, forcing the cruiser to hold fire for several minutes. Also at 0603, Leach turned sharply to port, assuming a course parallel to the Germans. During the next several minutes the German ships pummeled *Prince of Wales*. A 20.3-cm shell glanced off the base of the British battleship's forward 5.25-inch director

German battleship *Bismarck* firing on HMS *Prince of Wales*, as seen from the heavy cruiser *Prinz Eugen*, which is steaming ahead of *Bismarck*. (NHHC)

Prince of Wales sortied just seven weeks after commissioning. The ship was not worked up, she had many defects, and she sailed with dockyard workers still on board. The British could have paid a great price for their eagerness to concentrate superior forces against *Bismarck* and Captain Leech was wise to withdraw from the battle when he did. (NHHC)

without exploding but knocking both directors out of action. A 38-cm shell struck the starboard aircraft crane and exploded abaft the after funnel, blasting splinters across the boat deck and perforating the Walrus seaplane. A 20.3-cm round smashed a motor launch on the boat deck and plowed through the upper part of the ship, again without exploding: the crew threw it overboard after it came to rest in a shell handling room. A 38-cm projectile pierced the hull below the waterline without exploding but allowing four hundred tons of water to flood in. Finally, two 20.3-cm rounds struck and exploded below *Prince of Wales*' waterline, adding to the flooding.

At 0605, with the range down to 14,500 yards, Leach made another sharp turn to port, steering away from the Germans, who continued on course. At 0609, when the range was 17,000 yards, the British battleship made smoke and broke contact.

Prince of Wales had turned in a credible performance for a new ship that, by the end of the action, was limited to only two functioning guns (both of her four-gun turrets broke down). She fired eighteen main-battery salvos and five from her dual-purpose guns and hit *Bismarck* three times. One of her rounds pierced two tanks and isolated a thousand tons of fuel. Leaks left *Bismarck* trailing a long, iridescent ribbon of oil. The German battleship's top speed was reduced to 28 knots, and two thousand tons of floodwater in the forecastle had her down three degrees by the bow and listing nine degrees to port.

Bismarck had fired ninety-three 38-cm shells and an unknown number of 15-cm. *Prinz Eugen* fired 178 rounds of 20.3-cm and 78 rounds of 10.5-cm. On board *Prinz Eugen*, an after-action inspection revealed a metal fragment from *Prince of Wales*, apparently from an "over" fired at the time *Bismarck* passed her. This was the nearest she came to suffering any damage.

Painting by German artist Claus Bergen depicting *Prinz Eugen* (center) and *Bismarck* (left, distance) firing on British warships *Hood* and *Prince of Wales*. (NHHC)

At 1240 Lütjens turned south on a steady course at 24 knots. He had the whole Atlantic before him in which to vanish, but he decided that *Bismarck*'s steady loss of fuel required him to set course for St. Nazaire by the shortest possible route while *Prinz Eugen* hunted alone.

At 1839 *Bismarck* came about in a rain squall. *Suffolk* saw the maneuver on radar and was turning away when *Bismarck* emerged from the mist. The battleship fired at *Suffolk* from about ten miles; near misses loosened rivets aft but did no other damage. *Suffolk* replied with nine salvos, but these fell short. *Prince of Wales* and *Norfolk*, seeing *Suffolk* under attack, altered course toward the enemy. At 1847 *Prince of Wales* opened fire from about 26,000 yards, followed by *Norfolk* at 1853. However, Lütjens only intended to divert the British ships so that *Prinz Eugen* could break free for independent operations. The brief exchange of fire was over by 1856, although it was long enough for two of *Prince of Wales'* guns to malfunction.

After *Prinz Eugen* went her way Wake-Walker continued to follow *Bismarck*. Seven capital ships, two aircraft carriers, and twelve cruisers were converging on *Bismarck* from all directions. Her eventual destruction seemed a certainty.

The twists and turns of the *Bismarck* saga have been told many times. After the two ships separated, *Bismarck* successfully broke contact. The British found her again when Lütjens, not knowing he was free and clear, revealed his position by broadcasting a long report. The British, however, mistaking the bearing by 180 degrees, went off in the wrong direction. By the time they realized their mistake it would have been too late to catch *Bismarck* but for a lucky hit by a difficult aerial torpedo attack that jammed the battleship's rudder

and caused her to sail in circles. Two British battleships, *King George* and *Rodney*, at the very limits of their range, finally brought *Bismarck* to battle and sank her.

The story of *Prinz Eugen*'s subsequent actions is not so dramatic. She was free in the North Atlantic, and her priority was to disappear. She headed south into worsening weather and heavy seas. On the 25th she continued south. At 0653 she spotted smoke at a great distance and took action to avoid. At 0800 her fuel status was becoming worrisome, with stores at 1,145m^3. She expected to find the tanker *Spichern* in the mid-Atlantic at the latitude of Brest. By that evening the weather was moderating, but she had still not made

Manning the binoculars. (U.S. Naval Institute photo archive)

contact. She was reaching the limits of her endurance, and fuel was now the overriding concern.

On 26 May *Prinz Eugen* finally rendezvoused with *Spichern*. The cruiser was down to 250m³ of fuel oil, about 8 percent of her load. It took eighteen hours to refuel—a process the Germans did by trailing a fuel line from the tanker. Following this Captain Brinkmann resolved to turn back north into the HX convoy route. He explained, "It is possible that the Admiralty has drawn so many heavy units toward the direction of *Bismarck* that I may run into a quite lightly guarded convoy." Following this his future intentions were to raid south, always keeping his replenishment tankers nearby.

The British, as Brinkmann sensed, were indeed preoccupied with *Bismarck*, and rightly. They knew *Prinz Eugen* was somewhere out there on her own, and during daylight on the 26th, while the cruiser took on much-needed fuel, they thought they had found her. An aircraft that had been following *Bismarck* reported the battleship's position incorrectly, leading the Admiralty to conclude that it was really shadowing *Prinz Eugen* and that the cruiser was 60 miles south-southwest of *Bismarck*. This impression was reinforced by report from a Catalina flying out of Scotland at 0113 on the 27th

The ship's office. (U.S. Naval Institute photo archive)

of a ship on course 110 at 26 knots 350 miles west of Brest. *Bismarck* herself was well accounted for by this time. The natural conclusion was that this was *Prinz Eugen*, on her way to France, although at the time the German cruiser was west of the Azores 1,300 miles to the southwest of the French coast. Coastal Command searches of the mouth of the Bay of Biscay were intensified, and a large RAF strike force stood ready to fly once the cruiser's position was confirmed.

On the 27th *Prinz Eugen* failed to find the tanker *Esso-Hamburg* in the expected location. Then a message from Group West indicating a concentration of five British battleships caused Brinkmann to change his mind about raiding the HX-route. "A dodge to the north would bring me back under the air surveillance by the Americans and the English flying boats from Iceland." The captain also noted the need to attend to his engines. "The machinery urgently needs a few days' rest. The ship has been under continuous high performance since the 19th. If the installation is to perform as flawlessly as it has until now, it must be overhauled for a few days."

On the 28th *Prinz Eugen* found *Esso-Hamburg* and took on 680m³ of fuel oil. Captain Brinkmann resolved to refuel every day, "to be ready at all times for maximum cruising range." He decided to move his center of operations south and to position his tankers in the mid-Atlantic at the latitude of Casablanca. He felt that after the hunt for *Bismarck* had died down, he could pick off individual ships from that location, if he could prevent them from signaling his presence.

On 29 May, after transmitting elaborate orders to his supply and support vessels, Brinkmann abruptly decided to terminate his mission. A series of mechanical issues had been affecting the ship's performance. There was a leak in the main steam line that could only be controlled by dropping the pressure, thus affecting the capacity of the port engine. Next, the starboard screw was rumbling. This not only hampered the hydrophones but also prevented "overdue necessary overhaul work on the starboard turbine" because the starboard propeller shaft could not be uncoupled. Next, the main cooling-water pump amidships was acting up. There was no replacement pump on board, and if the pump should fail the center engine would have to be shut down. Finally, and most serious, the portside engine had suddenly failed. The shaft was disengaged, and an inspection found that some packing seals were smoking and bearings were dislocated. All repairs possible were carried out, but the engine continued to hum at 25 knots—not a good sign. Brinkmann felt that speed was his best defense and that without the ability to reach full speed, his mission was fatally compromised. During the day more failures occurred that caused Brinkmann to review the entire machinery status. He concluded that Turbine 1 (port) was "severely compromised," Turbine 2 (center) "only provisionally ready," and Turbine 3 (starboard) also compromised, by propeller damage. The boilers were judged capable of maximum performance, but the fuel received from *Spichern* was very contaminated, causing constant boiler failures. The doom-and-gloom tone of this assessment was clearly intended to justify beyond any shadow of doubt his decision to terminate the mission early, but likewise it is hard not to conclude that *Prinz Eugen* had little business undertaking a mission in which her success, indeed her safety, depended on mechanical reliability.

Prinz Eugen experienced a broad range of mechanical problems during her Atlantic cruiser, but at least the high-pressure boilers proved dependable. (U.S. Naval Institute photo archive)

All throughout the 30th and 31st *Prinz Eugen* sailed east at 29 knots (a feat of sustained high-speed steaming that suggested her machinery situation was not quite as bad as Brinkmann painted it). On the 1st she arrived in the Bay of Biscay, met the 5th Destroyer Flotilla, and at 1930 on the 1st reached Brest. She had steamed a total distance of 7,000 nautical miles over 14 days at an average speed of 24 knots. During this period she had consumed 6,410m³ of oil, nearly twice her capacity.

Ironically, the British finally located *Prinz Eugen* well inside the Bay of Biscay on the 1st, by direction finding from her radio transmissions. However, the cruiser's actual presence in France was not confirmed until the 4th.

In staff endorsements of Brinkmann's report, the commander of cruisers, Vice Admiral Huburt Schmundt, criticized *Prinz Eugen*'s performance at the Battle of Denmark Strait for failure to seek shelter immediately on *Bismarck*'s unengaged side. He stated that her guns could not have caused any real damage to enemy battleships and that her lack of armor protection made her a liability. He was perplexed that *Prinz Eugen* failed to fire torpedoes and described the gunnery officer's misidentification of the enemy battleships as cruisers as "incomprehensible." He did note, however, that the cruiser's shooting had been "exquisite." He also endorsed Brinkmann's decision to terminate the mission early. In contrast, the commander of Naval Group North, Admiral Rolf Carls, took the position that *Prinz Eugen*'s contributions to the Denmark Strait battle were valuable: she achieved hits, started fires, and forced the enemy to divide its own fire. "One cannot think only according to rules and must take chances in the exposure to danger." He also found Jasper's misidentification of the enemy perfectly comprehensible: "At very far distances, particularly at sharp angles, the identity of a ship's type . . . cannot be expected with absolute certainty."

Other than lessons learned, little had been gained by this mission, other than to establish a threat. The Germans did not attack a single Allied merchant ship, and the Kriegsmarine had lost the services of its largest warship. However, after *Prinz Eugen* joined *Gneisenau* and *Scharnhorst* at Brest, Raeder had a powerful squadron in an Atlantic port, and, as the British Admiralty feared, he remained eager to send his ships to sea.

SOJOURN IN BREST, JUNE 1941– FEBRUARY 1942

Stern view of German battleship *Gneisenau*. (NHHC)

Prinz Eugen entered drydock on 1 June 1941, immediately after her arrival in Brest. Prewar the Arsenal de Brest was the major Atlantic base of the French Marine Nationale. The extensive facilities included a 250-meter graving dock, occupied at the time by *Gneisenau*. In this port *Prinz Eugen* also joined *Scharnhorst*. Both battleships had been in Brest since their arrival on 22 March 1941 after their successful two-month cruise of the North and mid-Atlantic.

During their months in the Breton port the sister battleships had attracted much attention from British forces. Submarines established a patrol off shore, while on 24 March the British began laying a minefield to block the passage back up the English Channel. Bombing raids commenced with unsuccessful attacks on the nights of 30/31 March and 3 April. On 6 April, however, a Bristol Beaufort torpedoed *Gneisenau*. She entered dock on the 10th, only to suffer four more hits in a bombing attack that same night. These inflicted considerable material damage and killed eighty-eight men. This was the danger with Brest. Although the city gave German warships direct access to the Atlantic, it was only 140 air miles from Plymouth—an easy flight for a modern bomber. Moreover, while the port enjoyed excellent repair and support facilities, it was occupied territory; espionage and sabotage were constant worries. When damaged ships were under repair, work never progressed as fast or as well as it would have in Germany. Finally, arrangements for protecting the ships in port with antiaircraft batteries, fighter coverage, and camouflage arrangements were initially inadequate, although they were to become much better.

The British did not raid Brest in May, but after *Prinz Eugen*'s arrival attacks began again. Strikes on the nights of 7/8, 9/10, and 10/11 June delivered 200 tons of bombs and sowed mines off the harbor entrance. Two more raids that next week saw the bombers drop another 240 tons of ordnance. All these raids missed their targets and on board *Prinz Eugen*, covered by a massive camouflage net and with repairs to her engines nearing completion, perhaps there was a growing sense of complacency. If true, it was misplaced. The British enjoyed good intelligence of German activities in Brest and issued daily reports giving ship arrivals, departures, positions, and activities.

Gneisenau in drydock on a misty day. The guns in A turret are elevated, and camouflage netting obscures the foredeck. At the bottom is visible a bus used to transport crewmen to and from their barracks. (Koop and Schmolke)

46

At 2200 on 1 July, a calm and clear summer night, the alarm system cautioned the flak batteries that British bombers had taken off from Cornish airfields. German control stations plotted their course and at 0040 on 2 July intensified the alert and broadcast that Brest was the likely target. This caused sirens in town and in the port to begin howling and alarm bells and gongs to sound on the ships. Artificial-fog machines began spewing thick, chemical smoke; the crewmen welcomed the protection while at the same time gagging on the noxious concoction. As batteries around the port opened fire the glare from their gun flashes blinked redly through the fog. *Prinz Eugen*, as always, held fire so her weapons would not provide a point of aim. Nonetheless, on this particular night the first bombs fell close alongside, near the jetty, lifting geysers mast high and scattering stone

fragments on the cruiser's deck. At first all stations reported clear, and it seemed the ship had been nearly missed, but the control center did not report in. The reason became clear when the hatch that led from the control platform down to the control center opened and smoke poured out. Three men with blacked faces emerged, a sign that much worse waited below.

In fact, a bomb had penetrated *Prinz Eugen*'s armored deck and exploded in the gunnery transmitting station and gyrocompass room, inflicting severe damage. Splinters also perforated the ship's double bottom. Forty-seven men had been killed outright, including the ship's executive officer, and thirteen more eventually died of wounds.

The damage was such that the cruiser would spend another six months in dock, not emerging until 15 December. During this extended period workers added

(right) *Prinz Eugen* on 1 June 1941 entering Brest after her mid-Atlantic foray. (Koop and Schmolke)

(below) Brest harbor from the air, spring 1941. *Scharnhorst* is clearly visible in the center of the picture protected by an arched antitorpedo boom. *Gneisenau* occupies the first drydock to her left. (Koop and Schmolke)

Country and Place	Report	Date of Report

FRANCE (Contd

Brest

Much obscured by cloud. PRINZ EUGEN arrived
in Dry Dock since 31.5.41. SCHARNHORST and
GNEISENAU still present at usual berths.
1 M/V. 500/550 arrived Rade Abri, 2 M/Vs.
(200/250), 5 lighters, 4 barges left, 1 M/V.
350/400 arrived, 3 tankers 300' still present.   4.6.41.

SCHARNHORST, GNEISENAU and PRINZ EUGEN still
in same positions. 2 M/Vs. (200/250), 1 vessel
(150/200), left.
PRESENT SCHARNHORST, GNEISENAU, and PRINZ EUGEN,
1 Flak ship, 6 probable patrol craft, 1 S/M.
Redoubtable class 1 M/V (500/550), 1 M/V (200/
250), Salvage vessels 250', about 15 vessels (150/200),
about 20 barges and lighters.   7.6.41.

Only Port Militaire well seen. SCHARNHORST
left berth at T/B station and entered Rade Abri,
returned to former position later in the day,
bow pointing eastward. 3 probable auxiliary patrol
craft, 7 armed trawlers, 1 M/V. (350/400), left
and 1 M/V. (300/350), 4 vessels under 200' arrived.   9.6.41.

SCHARNHORST, GNEISENAU and PRINZ EUGEN still present.
1 M/V. (300/350), left Dry Dock No. 9. 1 M/V.
(400/450), 1 M/V. (300/350), left. 1 M/V. (400/450),
and 1 M/V. (350/400), apparently armed arrived.   10.6.41.

Brest (Contd)

SCHARNHORST, GNEISENAU and PRINZ EUGEN still
present. 2 auxiliary patrol craft arrived
making total of 5.
CHATEAULIN RIVER 2 S/Ms. Redoubtable Class
now present near hull of Cruiser DE GRASSE.
4 unidentified naval units (250/300), lying
alongside one S/M.   11.6.41.
SCHARNHORST, GNEISENAU and PRINZ EUGEN still
present. 1 M/V. 500/550 left. Vessel 400'
arrived Grand Bassin de Nord Est. Tanker 500/550
still present east of POINTE DES ESPAGNOLS   13.6.41.

British intelligence kept close tabs on the activity at every German port. This shows the information reported for Brest in the period of 4 through 13 June 1941, based mainly on photo reconnaissance flights. (NARA)

Prinz Eugen, heavily draped, sits in drydock, seen from the starboard side aft. Two French shipyard workers approach the camera. (U.S. Naval Institute photo archive)

Damage inflicted on the control center by the British in a 2 July 1942 bombing attack. Forty-seven men died immediately and thirteen more from their wounds. The damage required nearly six months to repair. (U.S. Naval Institute photo archive)

five quadruple 20-mm mounts and made several other small improvements. Although *Prinz Eugen* appeared to be the target on several other raids, she was not further damaged during her time in Brest.

Scharnhorst was ready for sea in July. On the 23rd she moved down the coast to La Pallice to reduce the number of targets in Brest. This attracted a raid by four Sterlings and then the next day by a dozen Halifax heavy bombers, which scored five hits and sent her back into dock at Brest. The Germans responded to these setbacks by basing more fighters around Brest, installing more smoke machines, and thickening the antiaircraft defenses. These measures forced the British to bomb at very high altitude or at night, with a consequent loss in accuracy. The British enjoyed good intelligence of the effectiveness of their raids, generally from "dockyard" sources that also kept them informed of the operational status of the ships. But this news tended to arrive late. For example, it took a month before intelligence confirmed the July hit on *Prinz Eugen*. The British also relied heavily on photo reconnaissance, making 729 sorties over Brest at the cost of nine aircraft from the time the first German battleships arrived.

After the deadly attack, most crewmen were barracked in the town. This shows a column of sailors marching to their accommodations. The ship herself dominates the background. (Koop and Schmolke)

Brest harbor taken from *Prinz Eugen*'s bridge. The destroyer *Z29* is on the left, and two other destroyers are anchored in the roads. A wood antitorpedo boom protects the ship. (Koop and Schmolke)

Despite the damage to *Scharnhorst* and *Prinz Eugen*, Raeder held hopes for completing repairs and having all three ships simultaneously ready for a sortie. On 25 July he explained to Hitler why surface ships needed to continue operating in the Atlantic.

The fact they are operating, or even just the possibility that they will appear in the Atlantic, supports submarine warfare to a great degree. If these [British] forces were free, they could operate with a very disturbing effect at other places, for instance, in the Mediterranean and in the Far East. . . . Moreover, the British would be able to strengthen their anti-submarine defences at the expense of the escort forces. . . . The fact that the British are making great sacrifices in order to keep the battleships from leaving port shows how much they fear the appearance of battleships on the ocean.

After a large attack at the beginning of August involving 149 aircraft, of which 16 were shot down, no attacks occurred until the week of 28 August. None of these raids harmed the Germans, although contemporary British assessments were hopeful, such as this one quoted from the Weekly Resumé provided to the British War Cabinet of 28 August to 4 September: "Over 85 tons of H.E. bombs were dropped on the docks at Brest, in which the battlecruisers *Scharnhorst* and *Gneisenau* are lying. Although a smoke screen covered the targets it is estimated that bombs burst in the area." In the next attack, which occurred on the night of 13/14 September, 120 bombers dropped 170 tons of bombs, but "searchlight dazzle and an effective smoke-screen" completely covered the target and the aircraft could not be sure they even hit the docks.

In his September conference with naval staff Hitler first suggested basing the heavy surface ships in Norway. Raeder reiterated that their best use was in the North Atlantic but that they would not be ready before 1942. In October Raeder stated the ships would be available in February and that short operations in the Atlantic were still possible. Hitler asked if they could

Two merchant vessels (some sources say three) were cobbled together and dressed in netting to resemble *Prinz Eugen* from the air and anchored along a quay to give British bombers a target. This photo shows the dummy ship being moved to its location. (U.S. Naval Institute photo archive)

Crewmen enjoying off-duty time with two tables of some three-handed card game. Their expressions all seem very serious. (U.S. Naval Institute photo archive)

be withdrawn through the English Channel. Raeder replied that perhaps *Prinz Eugen* could but not the battleships. In the face of the Fuhrer's insistence, he agreed to study the matter further.

After the large attack of 13/14 September, the Royal Air Force made in October seven scattered nuisance raids against the ships, dropping 103 tons of bombs in all. In November three raids delivered 200 tons. None of these attacks inflicted any damage.

In December, knowing that repairs on *Gneisenau* and *Prinz Eugen* were nearing completion, the British accelerated their aerial offensive. During the month the RAF made twelve attacks and dropped 545 tons of bombs. A German naval staff assessment made on 12 December cautioned that "further heavy attacks on Brest are to be expected. The enemy is determined to try everything to cripple our heavy vessels in order to enable British heavy vessels to proceed to the Far East." In response, the Germans continued to enhance the port's protection, transferring antiaircraft batteries from Germany. By 21 December the antiaircraft defenses included thirty-four heavy and twenty-two light batteries and nine searchlight batteries. Six fighter squadrons guarded the skies above the harbor.

As the German naval operations staff (SKL) war diary ironically noted: "The anti-aircraft artillery and pursuit plane protection is stronger than, for example, that of Wilhelmshaven." On 24 December the British Admiralty issued an alert that a breakout by the three ships was possible at any time.

The long spell of ineffectual raids ended on 18 December, when a bomb jammed the gate to *Scharnhorst*'s drydock and lightly damaged the battleship's hull. The yard estimated that a month would be needed before the ship could be undocked. This caused staff to lament, "Thereby enemy action has once again caused a very regrettable delay in operations to make this vessel fit for action." In fact, the raids created an exaggerated sense of peril. In one of his regular meetings with Hitler, held on 29 December, Raeder advised that *Prinz Eugen* would be ready in days and the battleships within a week or two but that it would take several months to train the crews and work up the ships. He recommended that once they were operational they undertake another Atlantic foray. Hitler, however, would have none of that. He firmly believed the British planned to attack northern Norway and that such an attack might be of decisive importance to the war's outcome. He wanted the ships transferred to the Arctic, and he wanted them to return to the North Sea through the Channel: "The only possibility is a surprise breakthrough." If this was not acceptable to the navy, then the Führer wanted their heavy guns removed to serve as shore batteries in Norway. Raeder, surprised and horrified, replied that more study would be required.

A study was duly made amid much angst within the naval staff and command, as well as the ships' captains. On 8 January a final opinion was formulated and presented in writing to Raeder. "All were *opposed* [emphasis in original] to plans for [withdrawal via the English Channel]. They particularly stress the fact that a transfer of the vessels from the Atlantic area, as well as the losses which are considered an inevitable consequence of such a move, must undermine our strategic and political position. [Withdrawal via the English Channel] is almost impossible unless grave losses are to be risked which would seriously hamper our conduct of the war." The navy's top minds conceded that assembling a strong naval force in northern Norway had operational and strategic possibilities, but they preferred maintaining an Atlantic presence. They all agreed that under no circumstances should the ships be disarmed.

The navy submitted a detailed opinion to Hitler on the 8th. This opinion included—as ordered—an outline plan for an English Channel breakout. The Führer's rendered his final decision on 12 January, rejecting, as expected, the navy's opinions and ordering the ships to return to Germany via the English Channel.

The decision to undertake the Channel passage home, as opposed to the longer route north of Britain, was not as dangerous as a glance at the map might indicate. On the oceanic passage there was the hazard of interception by the Home Fleet's battleships. The careful planning and organization that could be viably conducted for a two-day operation in the close waters of the Channel would not serve so well in the distant extremes of the perilous North Atlantic. Moreover, the crews of the three ships had been culled several times to provide personnel for submarines, torpedo boats, and other units. Their replacements needed training. A dash through coastal waters better suited their capabilities than would an oceanic voyage.

The camouflage netting disguising the dry-docked heavy cruiser. (Koop and Schmolke)

The British knew the ships were nearly ready to go, and in January they delivered on them a dozen attacks and 820 tons of bombs. Every bomb missed. Clearly the elaborate camouflage, artificial smoke, and strong barrages provided an effective defense. In fact, since the strike of 23 July the British had conducted thirty-nine attacks on the Brest dockyards and harbor, dropping more than a thousand tons of bombs, without scoring a single direct hit. The imperative to leave Brest was clearly not as great as the literature has made it appear. Nonetheless, the Führer had acted, and the German navy's surface strategy was dead.

THE CHANNEL DASH

THE GERMAN NAVY PLAYS THE BRITISH LION FOR A SPHINX, FEBRUARY 1942

O n 12 January 1942 Hitler ordered the return to Germany of *Scharnhorst*, *Gneisenau*, and *Prinz Eugen* via the English Channel. Because the operation required long nights and a new moon, the next (and best) opportunity would be a month away, during the second week of February. The three ships had been in port for a long time, and the skills of their crews had atrophied. Also, as newly repaired vessels they had trials to run and technical tests to undertake. Thus, training and other preparations intensified as the ships began leaving Brest each night to work up and exercise, returning before dawn. In one expedient, members of the antiaircraft crews of all three vessels were sent to the Baltic to train on board *Admiral Hipper* and *Admiral Scheer*.

Scharnhorst, flagship of the squadron breaking through the channel. This image shows her curved "clipper," or "Atlantic," bow to good advantage. The image was taken late 1939. (NHHC)

As the flotilla prepared, the German navy set in motion a series of activities across the span of coastline from Brest to the Jade River. Using the pretext that they were sweeping for a blockade runner, minesweeping flotillas began working in different sections of the English Channel to ensure the ships had a safe channel to follow; destroyers and torpedo-boat flotillas began moving west down the channel to be available as escorts when the breakout came. Even the destroyers that just escorted *Tirpitz* to Norway headed for France, leaving the battleship confined to her anchorage

Gneisenau taken during an Atlantic foray, probably early 1941. (NHHC)

for lack of escorts. The Germans paid extraordinary attention to security (six different code names were assigned to the operation, for example). Trucks brought loads of tropical equipment to the docks in Brest, and rumors were circulated that the ships were bound for the south, or would attack the Azores, or would even be making for the Indian Ocean. Everyone knew that something big was impending, they just did not know what.

Such activity could hardly escape British notice. Photo reconnaissance showed that the ships were exercising, and Enigma decryptions revealed that gun crews were working with other vessels. On 1 February, despite German efforts, the British Admiralty's Operational Intelligence Center, which knew the moon phases just as surely as did the Germans, opined that the ships would be departing Brest soon and that, while there was little evidence to show where they would go, a channel passage was most likely.

On 3 February the British began planning to counter such a move in an operation code-named Fuller.

Naval Group West crafted the plan for Operation Cerberus. Its most innovative feature had the ships depart Brest after dark. This would, the planners hoped, confound British expectations and delay their first sighting of the force. It was daring and dangerous, because it meant that the Germans would pass the Dover Straits at noon the next day. Hitler directed the

OPERATION FULLER

The British activated Operation Fuller on 3 February 1942. It was a combined navy–air force plan first devised in May 1941 to counter a movement by the German battleships from Brest up the English Channel. Fuller provided for certain air and naval units to be taken from their regular duties and reserved exclusively for striking a German force transiting the channel. It provided for a system of layered reconnaissance flights to give timely warning of the German movement. Air Surface Radar (ASV) equipped Hudsons would patrol two lines along the western reaches of the channel at night while during the day No. 11 Fighter Group would conduct two-plane sweeps of the channel between Fecamp and Ostend starting at dawn and every two hours thereafter. The planners assumed that the Germans would time their movement to pass the Dover Straits, the narrowest point in the channel, before dawn, when tidal conditions were most favorable and darkness would provide protection from shore batteries. The Admiralty diverted six destroyers from escort duties and held them in readiness at Harwich. Six MTBs waited at Dover and three more at Ramsgate while two submarines patrolled off Brest. The Admiralty also maintained six Swordfish of FAA 825 Squadron at Manston near Dover at immediate readiness. A dozen torpedo armed Beaufort fighters of Nos. 86 and 217 Squadrons were at Cornwall's St. Elav field ready to intervene if the Germans sailed into the Atlantic, while fourteen more of 42 Squadron were ordered south on 11 February. Bomber Command reserved 200 aircraft for Fuller and kept them at 2 hours' readiness. No. 11 Fighter Group likewise maintained squadrons at Thorney Island Field near Portsmouth at short notice in addition to its search responsibilities. The British expected to sight the enemy shortly after they rounded Ushant and to deliver the first wave of attacks west of Dover.

Another defensive measure taken by the British in the weeks before the breakout was laying of mines along likely evacuation routes. The minelayer *Manxman* worked out of Plymouth in the western channel; her sister ship *Welshman* operated from Dover; and Coastal Command dropped ninety-eight magnetic mines in previously swept channels and along the Dutch coast.

at all times. Air force flight controllers embarked on the three major warships. Elaborate minesweeping and a marked route would reduce that other great danger of sailing in contested coastal waters and permit the ships to steam at 27 knots. A strong force of destroyers, torpedo boats, and S-boats would screen the heavy vessels. The plan was tight, it was comprehensive, its practicality was leavened with a dash of imagination, and it was as safe as circumstances allowed.

The German force, led by *Vizeadmiral* Felix Ciliax, *Befehlshaber der Schlachtschiffe* (Admiral Battleships), flying his flag in *Scharnhorst*, departed Brest at 2114 on 11 February escorted by the 5th Destroyer Flotilla (*Beitzen, Jacobi, Schoemann, Ihn, Z25*, and its flagship, *Z29*) under the *Führer der Zerstörer, Kapitän zur See* Erich Bey. The departure was delayed nearly two hours because of an air alarm and occurred barely before the abort cutoff time of 2130. The night was dark and conditions good, and the weather was forecast to deteriorate the next day, as the Germans hoped it would. The fleet passed Ushant at 0012 on the 12th, seventy-two minutes behind schedule. British reconnaissance failed to detect the sailing. *Sealion*, the submarine posted to watch Brest, had withdrawn at 2035 to recharge her batteries, expecting the Germans would not sail at night. The Hudsons manning the first two search lines had malfunctions with their ASV radars, and the aircraft patrolling the third line missed the enemy.

By 0612 Ciliax was off Cherbourg, still undiscovered by the British and making up time lost by the delayed departure. Fighters began circling overhead beginning at 0645 (dawn was 0720) as the force continued east. According to a German account of the operation by Otto-Fritz Busch, "Morning came with brilliant sunshine, a steely blue sky and a dark green sea which gleamed blue in the distance as it did far out in the Atlantic."

At 0915 the 2nd Torpedo Boat Flotilla (*T2, T4, T5, T11,* and *T12,* under

Luftwaffe to cooperate. The German air force allocated 250 fighters to provide continuous fighter coverage, endeavoring to maintain at least 16 fighters overhead

Prinz Eugen's bow biting deep into Channel waters. (U.S. Naval Institute photo archive)

German torpedo boat with air cover close overhead. (U.S. Naval Institute photo archive)

Korvettenkapitän Heinrich Erdmann) from Le Havre and the 3rd Torpedo Boat Flotilla (*T13*, *T15*, *T16*, and *T17*, under *Korvettenkapitän* Hans Wilcke) from Dunkirk joined Ciliax. Still the Germans were unseen. British coastal radar detected circling aircraft near the French coast but interpreted this activity as some kind of rescue operation. Moreover, the Germans were jamming the British radars, degrading their effectiveness. At 1015 ten motor torpedo boats of the reinforced 4th S-boat Flotilla arrived as an outer screen. Their decks were painted luminous yellow to aid in aerial recognition. At 1025 *Scharnhorst* reduced speed to ten knots to lead the column through a minefield recently laid by the British and just discovered by the Germans. Minesweepers had barely cleared a narrow

channel when the squadron arrived. As the big ships carefully threaded this unexpected obstruction, two Spitfires flashed by overhead. The Germans had been at sea twelve hours; they were less than two hours' steaming time from the Strait of Dover. At last they had been sighted. Tension mounted on the bridges as the officers and crews anticipated that the enemy would respond to their presence with a massive attack. The Germans received another half hour of "grace," however, because the Spitfires maintained radio silence and reported seeing a large German convoy only after they had landed at 1109.

At 1047, having navigated the dangerous mined area, Ciliax increased speed to 27 knots, anxious to make as many miles east as possible before the inevitable

CHANNEL DASH

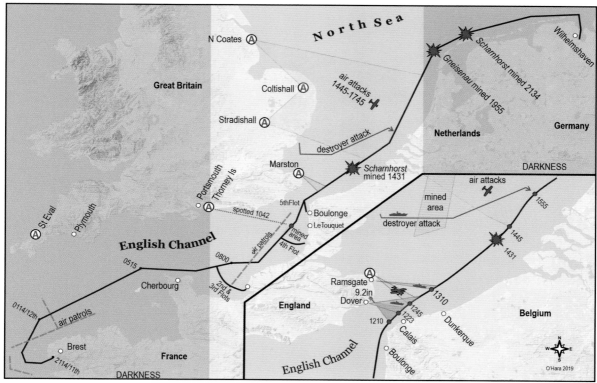

(Created by the Author)

Fleet panorama taken from the leading destroyer. Four torpedo boats in two columns are followed by *Scharnhorst*, more escorts, *Gneisenau*, and *Prinz Eugen* in the distance. This was probably taken around 1025 while the fleet was threading through a recently discovered and cleared minefield. (Koop and Schmolke)

attacks commenced. Meanwhile the 5th Torpedo Boat Flotilla (*Seeadler, Falke, Kondor, Iltis,* and *Jaguar,* under *Fregattenkapitän* Moritz Schmidt), rendezvoused off Cape Gris Nez near the narrowest portion of the Channel. It was 1133. Still no attacks.

In fact, the first alerts were just being sent. The Admiralty, which had received word from RAF channels, alerted the Dover command that the Germans were coming. Thus it was that the first British response to the German intruders came only at 1210 when shells from the 9.2-inch battery at South Foreland on the Dover Straits splashed into the water behind the German force. The battery fired thirty-three rounds from an initial range of 27,000 yards. All fell well short. Five Royal Navy motor torpedo boats (MTBs) cleared the Dover breakwater at 1155,

Crew members eating at battle stations. They seem happy with their small bowls of soup. (U.S. Naval Institute photo archive)

despite having been at four hours' notice and having been ordered out only twenty minutes before. The lead boat, *MTB 221*, reported contact with the enemy at 1223. None of the British boats, however, limited by a

top speed of 24 knots, could penetrate the screen of the escorting S-boats. They fired torpedoes from beyond the screen at ranges between three and five thousand yards. Two thousand yards or less was considered an effective range and the German fleet passed unharmed. A pair of motor gun boats (MGBs) arrived to support the MTBs but only after all torpedoes had already been expended.

The first air attacks started at 1245 when six Swordfish of 825 Squadron flew to their doom. Their slow speed—which mandated an immediate sortie—and the RAF's inability to supply the promised escort of five Spitfire squadrons at the time required meant that they approached the German force at 90 knots with only ten Spitfires in company. The leader, piloted by Lieutenant Commander Eugene Esmonde, who had achieved fame for heading the torpedo attack against *Bismarck* launched by the carrier *Victorious* the year before, was shot down within three thousand yards of *Scharnhorst*. German FW 190s splashed the five other

The Destroyer Attacks ADAPTED FROM *GERMAN FLEET AT WAR*

The German fleet had sailed largely unharmed through everything the British had flung at them; the last unit available to contest their passage was an amalgamation of the 21st and 16th Destroyer Flotillas: *Campbell* (flag of Captain C. T. M. Pizey), *Vivacious*, *Walpole*, *Worcester*, *Mackay*, and *Whitshed*. Of all the British units deployed that day, Pizey's flotilla was the most prepared. He had sailed from Harwich at 0600, long before the British knew the Germans were coming, and exercised his ships with an escort of six Hunt destroyer escorts thinking that if there were an emergency, he would be more available at sea than in

first the loss of *Walpole*, which stripped her main propeller shaft bearing and dropped out after 1320; then the British ships experienced a series of attacks delivered by British aircraft. *Walpole*, struggling to return to port, was attacked by a pair of Wellingtons even though she was far from where the German ships were supposed to be and bore a blue-white-and-red roundel on her forecastle. The aircraft missed well wide on their first pass and were circling to make a second bombing attack when a pair of FW 190s appeared and chased them off. The German fighters then patrolled over the British destroyer for a few minutes before disappearing.

four miles. The thick weather favored Pizey. An air attack was under way at the same time. He wrote: "great numbers of aircraft—friendly and hostile—were observed. Low down were large numbers of Me.109s and an occasional Beaufort; higher up were Hampdens, Dorniers and Me.110's while still higher a few Halifaxs were to be seen." The aerial show helped him penetrate the German outer screen undetected.

At 1542 the British destroyers turned to attack in two divisions: Pizey led *Campbell*, *Vivacious*, and *Worcester* against *Gneisenau*, while *Mackay* and *Whitshed* sailing to starboard of Pizey tried to obtain a

HMS *Campbell*, a World War I–vintage ship and one of the destroyers that attacked the German squadron. (U.S. Navy)

port. However, Dover command underestimated the German fleet's speed and by the time he realized their actual position relative to his own, Pizey could intercept only by steaming at 28 knots directly for the estuary of the River Scheldt in Holland across a presumed minefield. The Hunts could not participate as they were too slow to reach the contact point in time.

During their five hour run across the North Sea the destroyers suffered

A Hampden made two bombing runs on the main destroyer column near-missing *Mackay* and straddling *Worcester*.

Pizey pressed on undaunted. As the two flotillas neared the continental mainland, *Campbell*, the only ship equipped with modern T271 radar, acquired two large contacts 16,500 yards ahead. The time was 1517, and conditions were deteriorating with a heavy swell from the west and a rising gale; visibility had dropped to

firing position on *Gneisenau*'s bow. Pizey's three ships swung parallel to the battleship when the range was down to four thousand yards. One minute later *Z4* finally noticed the intruders and broadcast an enemy-contact alarm. She fired her guns and launched four torpedoes at *Campbell*'s column, one of which *Vivacious* barely avoided. *Z5* came up and shot six salvos and straddled her target; then both German destroyers cleared the range for the battleship and cruiser.

Gneisenau's large guns erupted with flame and smoke, but Pizey continued to close. His ship twisted between towering columns of water from 11-inch straddles until 1547 when, from a range of 3,300 yards, *Campbell* turned and fired six torpedoes; *Vivacious* on her starboard quarter fired three more. After their weapons were away *Campbell* (her bow damaged during her run in) fled to the northeast, shooting at enemy destroyers until 1553; *Vivacious* turned northwest. Both found shelter in a rainsquall. *Worcester* had been following about 1,600 yards back and missed her leader's turn; she pressed on for another three minutes.

Still heading up channel. Photographed from the heavy cruiser *Prinz Eugen*, with the battleship *Gneisenau* next ahead and the *Scharnhorst* in the distance. (NHHC)

Pizey claimed two of his torpedoes struck home, but in fact all missed. Meanwhile at 1543 *Mackay* and *Whitshed* saw *Prinz Eugen* steering toward them while avoiding a Beaufort's torpedo. At 1545 the cruiser realized the two ships were enemies and immediately opened fire. The range was less than four thousand yards. Smoke and the following wind forced the cruiser to pass gunnery control from the foretop to the forward director and the gun crews could only snatch glimpses of their targets as they appeared and vanished in the murk. *Mackay* launched torpedoes as soon as *Prinz Eugen* opened fire. *Whitshed* had trouble training her tubes due to

heavy beam-on seas that were washing over her deck. She did not launch until 1547, when the range was down to three thousand yards. *Prinz Eugen's* lookouts observed the British weapons entering the water and she swung south, allowing the bubbling wakes to pass ahead. Both British destroyers retired into a rain squall and returned to Harwich independently.

Worcester was the last ship to fire torpedoes. Her captain, Lieutenant Commander E. C. Coates, was determined to register a hit even though he was now in the crosshairs of both *Gneisenau* and *Prinz Eugen*. At 1550 with the range just 2,400 yards the destroyer swung to fire torpedoes. At just that moment two large shells

struck *Worcester's* boiler room. As the destroyer lost power she emptied her tubes under local control and drifted to a halt. Coates observed his torpedoes passing well behind the battleship and ahead of the cruiser. The cost of his unrequired boldness was heavy. During the next ten minutes six shells struck the helpless destroyer and she took on a heavy list as fires raged from stem to stern. As the German fleet swept by *Prinz Eugen* checked fire rather than waste ordnance on a ship obviously doomed, while a jammed shell case temporarily silenced *Gneisenau's* guns.

At 1558 *Campbell*, which had turned back, encountered *Worcester* lying stopped, "badly on fire forward and amidships, with smoke and steam pouring from the funnels, rafts and floats adrift clear of her and men in the water." However, after the Germans had disappeared to the north, her crew (those that had remained on board) extinguished her fires and worked up to 6 knots using salt water in the boilers. *Worcester* eventually returned to port under her own power having suffered twenty-seven dead and many wounded. She was out of action for fourteen weeks, while *Campbell's* damage required five weeks to repair. None of the other destroyers suffered harm even though the friendly air attacks continued as they returned to base.

Photographed from the heavy cruiser *Prinz Eugen*. *Gneisenau* is in the center, *Scharnhorst* in the distance to the left. (NHHC)

Another view of *Gneisenau* and *Scharnhorst* leading *Prinz Eugen*. (NHHC)

planes, although two managed to launch torpedoes at *Gneisenau*. One torpedo detonated upon hitting the water, and the battleship easily avoided the other. The British MTBs rescued five of the pilots and aircrew; the other thirteen died.

It was now 1300. The Germans were northwest of Dunkerque and emerging from the confined waters of the strait. Another hour and a half of sailing through rain and lowering clouds followed, uninterrupted until 1432 when *Scharnhorst* detonated a mine recently dropped by British aircraft. The ship lost all power, and her engines stopped. *Vizeadmiral* Ciliax hastily transferred to Z29 jumping on board the pitching destroyer as she scraped alongside. Four torpedo boats attended to the stricken battleship as the rest of the force swept on in accordance

with orders. Her situation looked dire—the double bottom was ruptured, and there was flooding—but the engines were not damaged. The engine room crew got a boiler back on line at 1449, and then a propeller shaft began turning, and within a half hour the ship was under way, working up to 27 knots. By that time the rest of the force was fifteen miles ahead.

As the Germans headed northeast along the Dutch coast the Royal Air Force finally began lifting off from fields in southeast England. By this time there was a low ceiling; it was raining, and the winds were picking up. The first RAF attack came in at 1445, and periodic strikes continued until dark, about 1745. Level bombers, especially those untrained in attacking naval targets under way, have a poor record of hitting warships, and

Fairey Swordfish, Royal Navy torpedo bomber. A squadron of these planes were destroyed trying to attack the squadron. (NHHC)

dropped his bombs from a thousand feet but saw no results. A German fighter damaged another Wellington. The squadron then returned, except for one aircraft that disappeared. Most reported: "Nothing seen after prolonged search." The squadron's log said: "The squadron had a very unsuccessful day and lost the Commanding Officer." Of the forty-eight attackers, twenty were lost, shot down or victims of the poor flying conditions. Fighter Command contributed 398 sorties at the cost of seventeen planes shot down. They claimed an equal number of Germans.

British destroyers attacked from 1543 to 1600 and launched torpedoes from relatively close ranges, helped by simultaneous air attacks and thick weather, but all for naught. Moreover, one destroyer was severely damaged, mostly by *Prinz Eugen*'s fire.

With dark, the Germans sailed past all British attacks but not away from all harm. At 1955 *Gneisenau* detonated a mine off Terschelling. This caused minor damage and the ship continued at 25 knots. *Scharnhorst* hit a second mine on 2134 and had trouble making port. *Gneisenau* and *Prinz Eugen* arrived at Wilhelmshaven at 0700 on the 13th. The Germans suffered only the loss of the patrol boat *V1302* to a bomb attack and light damage to *T13* and *Jaguar*. *Prinz Eugen* had one man killed in a strafing attack. During the operation she expended 157 20.3-cm, 230 10.5-cm, 640 37-mm, and 4,500 20-mm rounds. She hit *Worcester* several times, according to her own account. The British report does not specify the size of the six shells that hit *Worcester*, but given the damage inflicted, most were consistent with 20.3-cm rather than 28.3-cm shells.

- Starboard deck edge abreast the 12-pounder gun, which was put out of action

so it proved here. The RAF launched 243 bombers, 27 torpedo-armed Beauforts, and 18 Coastal Command Hudsons against the German fleet. The next day RAF command informed the British War Cabinet that "owing to poor visibility and low cloud, which was at times down to 500 feet, only 34 of the bombers and 14 Beauforts were able to attack." The experiences of 241 Squadron's Wellingtons can represent the whole. The squadron took off at 1445. One pilot believed he saw some German ships near the expected position off the Dutch coast. He

Prinz Eugen shipped several new quad *flakveirling* 20-mm antiaircraft mountings for this operation. (U.S. Naval Institute photo archive)

- Forecastle deck starboard, igniting 20-mm ammunition in a locker

- Forward boiler room, completely flooded and out of action

- After boiler rooms, temporarily out of action

- Paint room port side near stem, bulged starboard forecastle and upper deck some flooding

- Base of foremost funnel, port side, large hole and splinter damage

These blows also flooded the after magazine and shell room, put the radio out of action, and caused considerable splinter damage.

Strategically, the Channel Dash, as Operation Cerberus is commonly known in the English-language literature, was a major setback for the German navy. Never again would a ship larger than a destroyer be based in a French Atlantic port. Never again would the vital North Atlantic route between Great Britain and North America see surface warships ravaging a convoy. At the time, however, this was not apparent, and the event was perceived worldwide as a great victory for Germany, much as Hitler had predicted it would be. The public believed that the Royal Navy should have been able to control the English Channel and that its failure to stop the passage of a squadron was a defeat. It came at a time when the Allies were suffering setbacks on all fronts. In the Mediterranean, Malta was besieged and just a few days before, a resupply convoy had been completed defeated by Axis forces. The Afrika Korps had counterattacked in January 1942 and recaptured much of the territory taken by the British 8th Army in the November–December 1941 Crusader offensive. In East Asia, the Japanese were on Singapore Island and the fortress was clearly doomed. Another Japanese army was advancing through Burma. The Soviet winter offensive had ground to a halt. The Channel Dash came at a difficult time for the British and was naturally viewed in the worst possible light. As the 10 March edition of the *War Illustrated News* put it:

At 1:35 on the morning of Feb. 13 the Admiralty and Air Ministry issued a communique to the effect that the German warships *Scharnhorst* and *Gneisenau* and the 10,000-ton cruiser *Prinz Eugen*, accompanied by torpedo-boats, E-boats and mine-

Prinz Eugen's deck was littered with empty brass casings from her heavy antiaircraft and 20-mm gunfire. (U.S. Naval Institute photo archive)

sweepers, had been in action in the Channel with our aircraft and destroyers. The significant paragraph in the communique read as follows: "When last sighted, the enemy, which had become separated, were making for the ports in the Heligoland Bight."

It is hardly surprising that the British public were startled by this sensational, if brief, information. They had long been under the impression that the English Channel was inviolate, at least to German battleships. Further, as a result of 110 night and day bombing attacks on these ships, immured for nearly a year at Brest—Mr. Churchill disclosed on Feb. 17 that 4,000 tons of bombs had been dropped in the course of 3,299 bomber sorties, at the cost of 43 aircraft and 247 Air Force personnel—they had reason to think that the familiar S & G and the Prinz were hardly fit enough to take so long and hazardous a trip.

British consternation was matched by Axis elation. A German admiral broadcast, "For the first time for 250 years a fleet of an enemy of Britain has dared to enter the Channel." General Alan Brooke, Chief of the Imperial Staff, summed up the general feeling in his private diary: "News of Singapore getting worse, and that of Burma beginning to deteriorate! Added to that the *Gneisenau*, *Scharnhorst* and *Prinz Eugen* succeeded in running the gauntlet of the Channel yesterday without being destroyed, whilst we lost some 40 aircraft to the 20 enemy planes brought down! These are black days!"

NORWEGIAN INTERLUDE

PRINZ EUGEN DAMAGED IN NORTHERN WATERS, FEBRUARY–MAY 1942

Although *Scharnhorst* and *Gneisenau* sustained damage, the Channel Dash was a good operation for *Prinz Eugen*. Captain and crew alike were pleased with the cruiser's performance. The German command generously credited her with five aircraft shot down, at least one more probable, evading several submarine and destroyer torpedoes, and setting two enemy destroyers on fire and probably sinking one. The SKL War diary stated that she evaded "constant bomb and aerial torpedo attacks" although sailing alone and without aerial coverage. Once in Germany, she was immediately ready for her next task: Operation *Sportpalast*, redeployment to Norway.

Heavy cruiser *Admiral Scheer* at sea, en route to Norway in February 1942. Photographed from *Prinz Eugen*. Note the air recognition marking on the heavy cruiser's deck and the portable 20-mm antiaircraft gun mounting farther aft. (NHHC)

As originally conceived, Operation *Sportpalast* was to involve *Scharnhorst*, *Gneisenau*, *Scheer*, and *Prinz Eugen*. This fleet was to "carry out both offensive and defensive operations in the northern area." The Germans planned to transit the North Sea by day, relying on heavy weather to conceal their movement. The mine damage they suffered during Operation Cerberus meant that *Scharnhorst* and *Gneisenau* could not participate, which left just the two cruisers. They waited at the mouth of the Elbe for the right conditions and, given that it was winter on the North Sea, those conditions were not long in coming.

TO TRONDHEIM: OPERATION *SPORTPALAST*

At 0245 on 20th February, after just a week in German waters, *Prinz Eugen* edged into the North Sea from the mouth of the Elbe. She was serving as a flagship for Vice Admiral Ciliax. The admiral would transfer his flag to *Tirpitz* once he arrived. The heavy cruiser was also carrying 250 army personnel returning to duty from home leave. She led the armored ship *Admiral Scheer* and their escort, the destroyers *Beitzen*, *Jacobi*, *Ihn*, and *Z25*, and the torpedo boat *Seeadler*. They sailed into the German Bight and headed north.

The British were anticipating this movement, and Coastal Command was patrolling the North Sea. The German squadron was off the coast of Jutland 140 nautical miles into their journey when, at 1115

(Greenwich), a British aircraft reported two battleships and three cruisers, escorted by destroyers. The British immediately notified all submarines on patrol and ordered the Free French *Minerve* and *Trident* to take station off Christiansund. The Admiralty ordered: "Nothing smaller than cruisers is to be attacked." However, even though the aircraft reported five large ships, it also considered it improbable that the battle cruisers were present. The German signals intelligence detachment on *Prinz Eugen* took an hour to intercept and decipher the plane's report.

Upon receiving the bad news that they had been sighted, Group North ordered Ciliax back to the Elbe. Upon reflection, however and after consulting with Naval Staff, Group North changed its mind and instructed Ciliax to circle back north after dark. During their southward transit, a Lockheed made an unsuccessful torpedo attack on *Scheer* and was shot down by a German fighter. In its war diary, the German Naval Staff expressed the opinion that "the enemy was fully aware of the operation, because of the over-all situation and because numerous bits of information had leaked out." In fact, radio intelligence had alerted the British to the plan to move the heavy units north, and a spike in traffic tipped off the operation's date.

The British next sighted the German force at 0715 on the 22nd steering north off Stavanger. The Commander-in-Chief of the Home Fleet, Admiral John Tovey, sortied with the fleet and by midnight on the 22nd was two

Prinz Eugen's stern hanging at an angle after being struck by a submarine torpedo. She was able to make harbor in this condition and, fortunately for her, did not come under any subsequent attacks. (U.S. Naval Institute photo archive)

hundred miles west-northwest of Trondheim. *Victorious*, escorted by the heavy cruiser *Berwick* and four destroyers, intended to dash forward and launch a torpedo strike at 0100 on the 23rd before falling back to rejoin *King George V* and her escort. During this entire time the British carefully monitored the location of *Tirpitz*, sending out reconnaissance flights daily to ensure she remained in her berth near Trondheim.

The German squadron arrived at Bergen on 22 February and from there continued north at 2030. Admiral Ciliax counted on reports of low visibility for the 23rd to help screen his passage. Meanwhile, the British had concentrated the submarines *Trident*, *Minerve*, *Tuna*, and *P37* off Yrvefjord, which led to Trondheim.

The Germans had an uninterrupted journey north on the night of 22/23 March, through increasing seas, snowstorms, and decreasing visibility; *Beitzen*, *Ihn*, and *Jacobi* lost contact with the main force. Rather than continue independently to the final destination, they elected to return to Bergen. Thus, it was with a much-reduced escort that the heavy ships approached Yrvefjord. At 0551, as they were closing the coast, *Trident* spotted the German flotilla and maneuvered to fire torpedoes. Ciliax had reduced speed and was not zigzagging. Worse, the remaining escorts never spotted the low-lying submarine. *Trident* intended to fire a spread of seven torpedoes, the first three on the surface and the rest, in the face of the oncoming escort, submerged. However,

she only launched three, at 0702 from a range of 1,500 yards—because, through a failure in drill, a sailor moved a switch on the firing panel from "fire" to "stop fire." However, this was enough, as one torpedo caught *Prinz Eugen* in the stern and knocked off her rudder.

Originally, the Germans believed the cruiser had struck a mine. *Scheer* continued ahead at full speed and made Trondheim safely, leaving *Prinz Eugen* wallowing without power in a heavy sea amid a concentration of enemy submarines. But the cruiser soon managed to get under way at three knots, steering by her engines. *Tuna* spotted her after daylight but was unable to close. On the basis of signals intelligence, Group North radioed Ciliax that he had been attacked by a submarine and ordered the 2nd and 5th Torpedo Boat Flotillas out to assist the cruiser.

Scheer anchored in Trondheim at 1245, and *Prinz Eugen* arrived at Lo Fjord, northeast of Trondheim, at 2357 that same day. Thus, Operation Sportpalast was completed: a partial success at best.

Ciliax's preliminary report listed the major damage as:

1. Compartment I at scantling 6.5 is snapped off. Rudder jams at port 10. Rudder room is flooded. Steering engine in order.

2. Propellers are in order. Center and starboard shaft tunnels can be pumped out.

3. Both radar apparatuses and the UU device aft are out of order.

Prinz Eugen at anchor in Lo Fjord, a sheltered inlet of Trondheim Fjord. A torpedo boom protects the ship. The evening must be mild, as some of the loitering crewmen are not even wearing jackets. (U.S. Naval Institute photo archive)

The first requirement in patching up *Prinz Eugen* for a return to Germany was to cut away her damaged stern section. (U.S. Naval Institute photo archive)

This image shows a side view of the damage. The stern has been completely removed without harm to the propellers and is ready for the fitting of a temporary rudder. (NHHC)

4. Losses among the crew: 1 seriously and 12 slightly wounded; so far 2 are missing.

5. Losses of men on leave: 5 dead, 1 seriously and 12 slightly wounded.

With *Scharnhorst* and *Gneisenau* already in dock, this blow to *Prinz Eugen* was a major setback to Germany's plans for a strategic redeployment to Norway.

It was immediately clear the *Prinz Eugen*'s damage was too great to be repaired in Trondheim. She needed to jury-rig a rudder to enable her to venture out for the dangerous passage back to German waters. This involved the construction of a temporary rudder in Kiel and shipping it to Trondheim. It arrived on 21 April, and fitting it on the cruiser took until 9 May.

Although the decision to return *Prinz Eugen* for permanent repairs had been made from the first, the Germans had other alternatives. On 1 May Group North recorded the following opinion:

Units of the fleet in the northern area serve to exert strategic pressure and to prevent landings. Strategic pressure, due to lack of oil, is exerted merely by

This photo shows the new rudder being fitted to the *Prinz Eugen*'s chopped-off stern. (U.S. Naval Institute photo archive)

In other words, considering the ships had no oil, a damaged *Prinz Eugen* was almost as good a deterrent as an operational ship. This was a realistic attitude, but Naval Staff in Berlin disagreed and insisted on a policy of restoring damaged vessels to full combat readiness as quickly as possible.

THE RETURN: OPERATION *ZAUBERFLÖTE*

Prinz Eugen got under way at 0430 on 16 May. She was capable of 31 knots but was slow to respond to the helm, and her turning radius was twice normal. Her escort for the voyage south consisted of destroyers *Z25* and *Jacobi* and torpedo boats *T11* and *T12*. Both destroyers were going home for dockyard refits.

Reconnaissance aircraft first spotted *Prinz Eugen* while she was still in the Trondheim Leads, and the British kept a close watch thereafter. Between 1039 and 1905 on the 16th the air control center reported twenty-three separate sightings of enemy aircraft. No attacks developed that day, however, as the heavy cruiser threaded its way through the inner passages of

the presence of the ships. . . . The risk involved in transferring two heavy naval vessels during the season of the long days and considering the submarine conditions off Trondheim is considered a great one by the Group. Compared to it the disadvantage caused by the delay in putting the *Prinz Eugen* in combat readiness is of minor importance.

Dönitz and the Strategic Purpose of Norway

(ADAPTED FROM *HITLER'S ADMIRALS* BY G. H. BENNETT AND ROY BENNETT, NAVAL INSTITUTE PRESS)

"The main sphere of activity of the remaining heavy units of the fleet had now moved to Northern Norway, where new tasks awaited them. From the general strategic point of view our main interest lay in further immobilizing as large a part of the English fleet as possible in English home waters, thereby relieving both the Mediterranean and the Far Eastern theaters of war. The Anglo-American convoys to Murmansk and Archangel that had meanwhile come into operation represented an objective of equal strategic importance which was attacked by our naval forces at different times with varying success, while U-boats and aircraft operating jointly frequently achieved considerable successes."

However, Admirals Otto Schniewind and Karlgeorg Schuster, at the time fleet commander and commander of Group South, respectively, noted that aerial

cooperation remained the black hole of German naval operations:

"Naval operations from Norwegian bases, including those undertaken by U-boats, were very much hampered by the weakness of our own air force, which could place few aircraft at our disposal for naval operations. In this area the air force's insufficient support of the navy was particularly in evidence. Not only for the operations themselves was there no satisfactory reconnaissance or fighter support, but at the bases and in the inshore routes no really strong fighter protection was assured or it was given only for special operations of limited duration in a designated area. In spite of this, however, no severe losses occurred in the course of 1942. Cooperation with the reconnaissance units improved through practice in the course of the year but their strength never rose to a satisfactory figure."

Norway's fjord-riven western coast. With *Lützow* also at sea heading north, the RAF readied for action Coastal Command's two Beaufort torpedo-bomber squadrons: 42 Squadron, based at Leuchaurs, Scotland, was to attack *Lützow*, but upon hearing that the enemy ship had reversed course, it stood down. Meanwhile, sixteen Beauforts of 86 Squadron, based at Wick, took off just after midnight to intercept *Prinz Eugen* off Stadlandet, an exposed section of coast where the ship had to transit a stretch of open sea before regaining the shelter of the offshore archipelagos. The bombers missed their target, although the ship's lookouts sighted some of them from long range.

Prinz Eugen was next reported off Karmøy, north of Stavanger, midafternoon on the 17th; the RAF responded with a two-pronged attack in a determined effort to sink the elusive cruiser. Twelve Beauforts of 42 Squadron got airborne, escorted by four Beaufighters and six Blenheims. From 86 Squadron took off fifteen Beauforts, with an escort of four Beaufighters. Finally, a high-level bombing force of twelve Hudsons took off for the Norwegian coast,

(top left) The ships in Norway were subject to periodic attack by the RAF and Fleet Air Arm (FAA). This image shows two British airmen who had been shot down and rescued being brought on board *Prinz Eugen*. (U.S. Naval Institute photo archive)

(top right) In any ship, in any port (but especially in a foreign port) the receipt of mail is one of the most welcome events in a sailor's routine. (U.S. Naval Institute photo archive)

(left) The German passion for training extended to nonnaval activities. Here a landing party is practicing infantry tactics. (U.S. Naval Institute photo archive)

(right) The stereoscopic range finder used on German warships had the advantage of being able to acquire a target quickly. It had the disadvantage of being difficult to use and required a highly skilled operator, who had to resolve the two images—a skill that required practice. Here teams are using small range finders to maintain their skills. Note that each man with a range finder has a partner who is noting down information. (U.S. Naval Institute photo archive)

Prinz Eugen returned to Germany with a temporary rudder fitted to her chopped-off stern. The rudder was adjusted by men turning the capstan. Naturally, she was slow to respond to the helm, and her turning radium was huge, but the expedient worked. (U.S. Naval Institute photo archive)

The 1942 Fuel Crisis in Norway

EXTRACTED FROM U.S. NAVY DEPT., *SPECIAL REPORT ON OPERATIONS AND ORGANIZATION OF THE GERMAN NAVAL SUPPLY SYSTEM DURING WORLD WAR II*, 20 MARCH 1953.

In a report on the marine fuel oil situation made by Grand Admiral Raeder to Hitler in early 1942, CinC Navy stated that the Italian Navy was in continual need of fuel and that the Navy's stocks were running low. The passage of the Brest group through the Channel and onto Norway, he said, consumed 21,000 tons of fuel oil alone. By April 1st, he continued, the Navy's reserve stocks had dwindled to 150,000 tons, Roumanian deliveries fell from 46,000 tons to 8,000 tons per month and, since that had been promised to the Italians, who urgently needed fuel for the Mediterranean campaign, further withdrawals had to be made from Navy stocks. He complained: "The total allocation of black fuel oil for both the German and Italian navies for April (1942) has been cut from 97,000 to 61,000 tons." This cut, however, did not affect pocket battleships

or submarines, because both of these types of vessels used diesel oil.

Study of CinC Fleet's files discloses that in February 1942 the fuel oil situation in Norway was critical. A minimum monthly quota of some 5,000 tons was required for vessels, torpedo boats and destroyers stationed in or transferred to that theater, and this only for normal harbor routine, anti-aircraft readiness and two training voyages a week in the fjords.

This figure therefore excluded the transfer of ships or operational requirements. A further transfer of ships, commencing mid-March, made it necessary for the Fleet Command to request replenishment of fuel oil stocks in Norway.

Naval Group Command North reported that the fuel oil situation was critical in the whole of its area of its function being to attack the German airfield at Sola just outside of Stavanger. The plan of attack called for 42 Squadron to make landfall 50 miles south of Mandal and then to sweep northwest toward Lister, while 86 Squadron was to sweep southeast from Stavanger with the intention of executing a pincer attack on the damaged cruiser. A Beaufighter shadowed the German squadron to guard against any doubling-back tricks, but the BF 109s covering the cruiser attacked it; the Beaufighter reported a position that was too far north. Nonetheless, 42 Squadron sighted the enemy at 2015, earlier than it expected from the incorrect position report. The weather was good, visibility excellent, and the sky clear.

On the German side, lookouts reported the enemy approaching at 2008. One observer described it as being "like a swarm of starlings rising and falling." The cruiser fired four rounds from B and C turrets, set to splash ahead of the approaching line of aircraft. *Jacobi* reported torpedo tracks to starboard and fired warning flares. According to *Prinz Eugen*'s account the cruiser also sighted tracks, mistaking them for submarine torpedoes because the aircraft did not appear to be in a position to attack effectively. As the range quickly closed, the medium and then light flak opened fire, and the escorts contributed to the barrage. The six

escorting fighters and the ship's Arados were vectored to the wings of the attacking formation. The cruiser turned to present her stern to the enemy and rang up emergency full speed. The crew of D turret manned the steering capstan as if their lives depended on it. The ship stopped the starboard engine to accelerate the swing to starboard. The torpedoes ran alongside the cruiser as she successfully combed the spread of six weapons.

The second wave of Beauforts attacked from the starboard side. Once again, the ship commenced a series of broad turns as it weaved its way through the oncoming tracks. When it appeared that the two torpedoes would intersect the ship's bow, Captain Brinkmann ordered engines emergency full astern. Reportedly he instructed the navigating officer how to keep the knees flexed to absorb the shock of impact. This proved unnecessary, as both weapons crossed ahead of the ship. Twelve minutes after it had all begun, the enemy aircraft had disappeared, leaving the ship's crews jubilant at their escape and counting the number of aircraft destroyed. *T12* claimed two, *Prinz Eugen* six, and the ship's aircraft one. In fact, only three of the Beauforts were shot down, and one of the Beaufighters ditched on the way home. The Germans rescued the squadron commander, whose aircraft was one of the three.

---

command (i.e., Germany, Denmark, Finland and the Baltic States). Only small stocks were available. SKL had arranged for the transfer of stocks from France and the Lowlands. At the end of January 1942, about 140,000 cubic meters of fuel oil were stored in France and the lowlands. Adm Qu III [sic] had arranged for 50,000 cubic meters (314,386 U.S. barrels) to be carried via the inland waterways and by rail, so as to avoid the dangers of the sea route. Group North had requested four large and two medium fully-laden tankers from French waters, because of the shortage of tankers in waters around Germany. At the end of March 1942 SKL informed the Naval Group Commands and the Fleet Command that, because of the fuel oil crisis and the necessity for holding fuel oil reserves for the Italian Navy's urgent convoys to North Africa, it had become necessary to further reduce oil consumption. Operations by heavy naval units which consumed fuel oil were to be suspended. Commands were to get along on existing quotas, so as not to restrict operational freedom still further by premature consumption of already small stocks. It was, however, emphasized that necessary

operations, occasioned by offensive operations of the enemy, were to be carried out without regard to quotas. In such events, the amount consumed above the quota was to come from stocks and could not be replaced. At the beginning of April 1942, SKL ordered that even operations by light naval forces requiring fuel oil were to be suspended. The reason was an unexpected reduction in supplies of oil from Roumania. In May 1942, the fuel oil crisis had reached the stage where the Fleet Command reported that the cruiser "LUETZOW," the destroyers and the torpedo boats would be put out of commission unless an additional 6,000 tons of fuel oil were sent for May. In 1942, all hope for success in naval operations hinged upon the oil situation. In November 1942, CinC Group North cabled to the Fleet Command that SKL had given its approval for the cruiser HIPPER and four destroyers, together with the cruiser KOELN, if necessary, to make a sortie against the convoy QP-15. Fuel oil was to be taken from the reserve saved from the training allocation, estimated at 1,500 tons, or was to be drawn from the December quota.

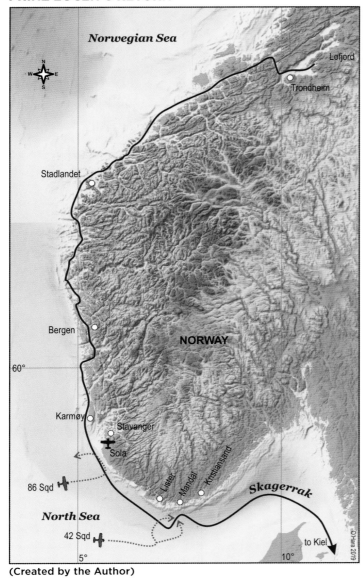

(Created by the Author)

by their success calling it "a splendid success of the ship's defenses and her fighter escort." According to their assessments forty aircraft attacked; they claimed twenty-two aircraft shot down by fighters, seven by ship's flak, and four by air force flak. In its weekly report to the War Cabinet the RAF stated, "The first force was unable to locate the cruiser [the 86 Squadron's 16 May sortie] but part of the second force [42 and 86 Squadrons], which consisted of 52 aircraft, including 27 torpedo-carrying Beauforts, carried out an attack. Two possible hits with torpedoes are claimed. Considerable enemy fighter opposition was encountered and nine of our aircraft failed to return. Five enemy fighters were destroyed. The *Prinz Eugen* has since been identified by photographic reconnaissance as having arrived at Kiel." This was the first mass Beaufort attack of the war (the aircraft had achieved one success against *Lützow* in June 1941), and the aircraft had again failed to realize the promise that a fast torpedo bomber offered as an effective weapon against ships at sea—a promise that, as of May 1942, only the Japanese and the Italians had begun to realize. It was still a matter of training and experience.

The return of *Prinz Eugen* to Germany was a triumph in the sense that it extracted a seriously damaged vessel from an exposed position and defeated a large air attack along the way. Given Germany's overall situation, however, the decision to put the cruiser in Norway in the first place was questionable, because in 1942 the German navy was experiencing a crisis in its fuel oil supply. This crisis rendered the fleet painstakingly gathered in Norway virtually worthless. Warships have a certain value in just their presence; this is why a fleet-in-being (that stays in port and exercises power solely through the possibility it might sail) can influence an enemy's actions. But, over the course of a war a ship that cannot sail because it lacks the means—a trained crew or even the oil to fire its boilers—is ultimately worthless.

Sitting at the end of a very long line of supply, the German fleet in Norway was little more than a paper tiger.

After the attack, a pair of Hudsons bombed the force from high level, missing astern by three to four thousand yards. Eighty-six Squadron was confused by the scout's incorrect position report and turned north (instead of south) along the coast, running into German fighters out of Sola, which shot down five Beauforts. The remaining aircraft reached home without having sighted their target at all. *Prinz Eugen* expended four 20.3-cm shells, 361 rounds of 10.5-cm, 486 37-mm and 2,082 20-mm rounds during this twelve-minute action, more than she used during the entire Channel Dash. The Germans were elated

PRINZ EUGEN REPAIRED AND IN THE TRAINING SQUADRON

CRUISERS AT WAR IN OPERATION RAINBOW, MAY 1942–JANUARY 1944

(left) Shipboard routine continued after the return to Germany. An ordinary sailor with a drawn bayonet stands guard next to the flag of honor visible in the glass case to his left. This is the crown of St. Stephen above a red, white, and red emblem. These symbols occupied the center of a red, white, and red horizontal tricolor—the colors of the old Austro-Hungarian flag.

(right) Galley duty: the badge on the arm of the man receiving the soup indicates he belongs to the Line Division and is a seaman 1st class with fewer than 4.5 years of service. (U.S. Naval Institute photo archive)

Upon her arrival at Kiel on 18 May 1942 *Prinz Eugen* was assigned to the training squadron. Work parties removed all her ammunition, and the ship moved into No. 5 Dock at Deutsche Werke. After inspection the yard estimated that repairs would require three and a half months.

On 31 July Captain Brinckmann left *Prinz Eugen*. He was promoted to rear admiral and appointed chief of staff of Group South. Clearly, his command of the heavy cruiser had pleased his superiors. His replacement was Captain Hans-Erich Voss. Voss' last stint at sea had ended in March 1938 as the first gunnery officer on *Admiral Graf Spee*. His entire war career since had been in staff positions. His time on *Prinz Eugen* was relatively brief before being appointed as naval liaison to the Führer headquarters in March 1943. He went on to survive the 20 July attempt to assassinate Hitler and reportedly was the last person to see Hitler and Goebbels alive before they committed suicide.

Air raids and a shortage of workers delayed repairs on *Prinz Eugen* (much the same situation as in Brest). Nonetheless, on 20 October she was once again ready for sea, and ammunition was loaded. The plan had not changed: Norway was the cruiser's ultimate destination. On 27 October she set sail for Gotenhafen. Throughout the autumn the ship trained her crew and worked up.

OPERATION *FRONTTHEATRE*

Operation *Fronttheatre* involved the transfer of *Scharnhorst* and *Prinz Eugen*, united again, to Norway. *Scharnhorst* flew the flag of Fleet Commander (fleet commander-in-chief) Admiral Otto Schniewind. They departed Gotenhafen on 9 January 1943 and passed through the Belts on 11 January. The weather was fair and cloudy. Eight FW 190s flew air cover. At 1306 an enemy aircraft was briefly sighted, and a minute later B-Dienst intercepted the plane's sighting report. Thirty minutes later the Germans intercepted a second sighting report.

The Home Fleet sortied, intending to intercept the German squadron off the coast of Norway. However, late that afternoon Schniewind reversed course, and *Prinz Eugen* returned to Gotenhafen. The German command decided to wait until the commotion died down and then try again.

OPERATION DOMINO

On 23 January *Scharnhorst* and *Prinz Eugen* again sailed for Norway. British aircraft sighted and reported them on the 25th, causing Group North to abort their mission once again. *Prinz Eugen* returned to Gotenhafen. This would be her last attempt to reach northern waters: she would spend the rest of her war in the Baltic. In part this was because events at the end of 1942 and the beginning of 1943 affected the deployment and use of

On 22 November the Italian *Contrammiraglio* Carlo de Angelis inspected the ship and during the occasion presented the crew with bell from the Austro-Hungarian battleship *Tegetthoff*. This was originally to have been the ship's name, and the gift represented Italy's acceptance of *Prinz Eugen*'s association with her old maritime enemy, the Austro-Hungarian Royal and Imperial Navy. (NHHC)

Germany's heavy surface forces. In the Battle of the Barents Sea, fought on 31 December 1942, a strike force that included *Hipper* and *Lützow* intercepted an Allied convoy bound for Russia but failed to achieve a decisive result. Unfortunately for the navy, preliminary reports had led Hitler to expect a great victory. As it turned out, not only was the result much less than that but the news was greatly delayed in getting to him—and when it did arrive, it came from the BBC. The Führer flew into one of his famous rages. He called the delayed report a "colossal insolence" and declared that the action showed "that ships were completely useless."

When Grand Admiral Raeder and Hitler had their next conference on 6 January 1943, Hitler subjected the admiral to a ninety-minute harangue blasting the navy's history and performance and ordering him to consider where the heavy guns of the ships could be mounted on land and in which order the ships should be decommissioned. This was too much for Raeder, who submitted his resignation as of 30 January.

Admiral Karl Dönitz replaced Raeder. Although certain ships were retired, most notably the crippled *Gneisenau*, he ultimately softened the Führer's resolution to pay off the fleet; most of the modern heavy ships remained in service. In his 26 February meeting, for example, Dönitz got Hitler to agree that "instead of decommissioning *Tirpitz* and *Scharnhorst*, [Dönitz] would consider it his duty to send them into action whenever possible and as long as suitable targets could be found." The impact on *Prinz Eugen* was that her orders for Norway were rescinded. On 28 February Captain Voss was replaced by *Kapitän zur See* Werner Erhardt, who had been a staff officer prior to this assignment. Under his command the cruiser embarked four hundred naval cadets in April 1943 and throughout the bulk of 1943 engaged in training activities in the Baltic as a part of the training command, under *Vizeadmiral* August Thiele.

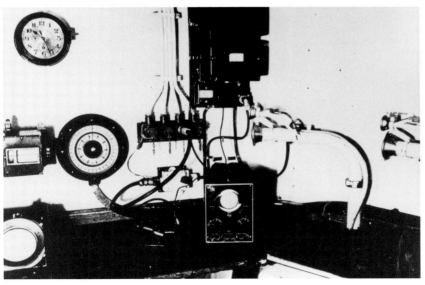

(top) FuMB Ant. 4 (Sumatra) radar search receiver antenna, fitted to the ship in February 1942. These are broadband diagonal antennas, four of them arranged so that one faces each quadrant of the ship. They were used with the Borkum-Naxos combination equipment shown in the photo below. (NHHC)

FuMB 10-FuMZ 6 (Borkum-naxos) radar search receiver combination housed in the fleet staff information central room. This equipment used the four Sumatra antennas atop the forward superstructure. The four plugs on the bulkhead are for switching antennas. (NHHC)

OPERATION RAINBOW

EXTRACTED FROM *GERMAN FLEET AT WAR*

The activity log of Germany's High Seas Fleet during the summer of 1942 made a thin volume. The capital ships shifted from anchorage to anchorage to confuse British attacks; the shortage of fuel oil limited their training and the enforced idleness degraded both morale and effectiveness. Moreover, Hitler had decreed that before he would condone a convoy attack by the surface fleet there had to be a weak escort with no aircraft carrier or heavy ships and a

U-boat shadowing. These were tough conditions to meet.

There were only two operations that summer. In August *Scheer* briefly cruised into the Kara Sea. She missed a nine-ship convoy but on 25 August sank the Soviet icebreaker *Alexander Sibiriakoff* after "heroic resistance," and shelled the port of Novy Dikson, damaging the icebreaker *Dezhnev* and the steamer *Revolutsioner*. On 24–28 September *Hipper* and five destroyers successfully mined the lonely waters

off Novaya Zemyla. Between October and December 1942 thirteen Allied freighters sailed to the Soviet Union independently. Only four arrived. On 5 November *Hipper* with *Z4*, *Z16*, *Z27*, and *Z30* swept the Barents Sea in search of this traffic and enjoyed a small success when *Z27* sank the Soviet trawler *SKR23/Musson* and the tanker *Donbass* on 7 November.

After the Battle of Stalingrad, it was clear the Soviet Union had survived another year. With the resources freed up after the North African landing, the British began planning to renew their Arctic convoys to the Soviet Union.

At 0300 hours, 30 December 1942 *U354* reported a lightly guarded convoy of six to ten ships fifty miles south of Bear Island. She had found JW51B which originally consisted of fourteen freighters escorted by the destroyers *Onslow* (flag, Captain Robert St. Vincent Sherbrooke), *Oribi* (which lost contact before the battle and did not participate), *Obedient*, *Obdurate*, *Orwell*, *Achates*, the minesweeper *Bramble*, the corvettes *Hyderabad* and *Rhododendron*, and two trawlers, *Ocean Gem* and *Vizalma*. JW51B was a test of Tovey's theory that two small convoys would be easier to protect than a single large one. JW51A had sailed a week earlier and arrived in Soviet waters unnoticed; so far so good, but JW51B had a rougher time. On Christmas Eve a powerful storm scattered the ships and one week later there were still stragglers.

U354's report excited Naval Group North: at last a target which met all the Führer's prerequisites. That same morning they ordered the polar fleet

A German Type VIIC submarine on patrol in the Arctic Sea, north of Norway. (NHHC)

UNITED STATES NAVAL INSTITUTE

The captain of *Admiral Scheer* addresses the crew gathered on the after deck concerning their forthcoming offensive cruise in the Barents Sea, August 1942. (NHHC)

to stand by. Initially only *Hipper* and six destroyers of the 5th Destroyer Flotilla under *Kapitän zur See* Alfred Schemmel, *Beitzen*, *Riedel*, *Eckholdt*, *Z29*, *Z30*, and *Z31*, were to participate in the planned action, but Berlin gave permission for *Lützow* to join the force at the last moment (she received the final confirmation of her orders after she was already underway).

Kummetz's plan called for *Hipper* and three destroyers, *Eckholdt*, *Beitzen*, and *Z29*, to approach from the northwest and attack at dawn (0840 hours) attracting the convoy's escorts. He assumed the convoy would turn south where *Lützow*, *Riedel*, *Z30*, and *Z31* would be waiting to snap it up. Daylight at that latitude and time of year consisted of four hours of twilight. For all ships to arrive at the right place at the right time would require careful coordination and good luck. After the engagement *Lützow* was to conduct a raiding cruise in the Arctic Ocean. (*Kapitän zur See*

Rudolf Stange, *Lützow's* captain, only learned of this mission after he was at sea!) Kummetz's orders were typically restrictive—he was to avoid action with equal or superior forces and not risk his heavy ships in a night action.

Leaving the sheltered waters of Altafjord the fleet encountered a heavy swell which laid many low with seasickness. *Lützow*, for example, was two hours decoding instructions from Kummetz because her signals staff were all sick. To ensure he found his target in plenty of time Kummetz sailed in an extended line of search eighty-five miles long with *Hipper* at the northern end and *Lützow* at the south. Between the cruisers, in order from north to south, sailed *Z16*, *Z29*, *Z4*, *Z31*, *Z30*, and *Z6*.

The British had four groups of ships scattered in the vicinity, none of which knew for certain the exact position of the others. The convoy—now twelve ships with eight escorts—was heading east. Forty-five miles north the trawler

Vizalma was playing shepherd to one straggler while *Bramble*, fifteen miles northeast of the convoy, was searching for the other. Finally, Force R, *Sheffield* and *Jamaica*, commanded by Rear Admiral Robert Burnett, sailed fifteen miles southeast of *Vizalma*. *Hipper* and her destroyers were rushing north toward their attack position while *Lützow* and her destroyers were fifty miles south and closing. There was a low overcast, scattered snow squalls, a calm sea and good visibility seven miles to the north and ten miles to the south. A gentle breeze blew west-northwest at 16 knots.

Fortune initially favored the Germans. At 0718 hours, in the Arctic pre-dawn darkness, *Hipper* detected shadows to starboard. She pulled back and sent *Z16* to investigate. More shadows emerged. Kummetz had found the convoy. Dawn was an hour away. His ships were in perfect position. Operation Regenbogen was off to a good start.

At 0820 *Hyderabad*, sailing on the convoy's starboard quarter, sighted two vessels, but did not report them assuming Soviet ships had joined the escort. At 0830 *Obdurate* on the starboard beam saw the same two ships bearing 210°. She informed Captain Sherbrooke who sent her to investigate.

Obdurate followed the contacts (Z16, Z4, and Z29) around the stern of the convoy and off to the northwest. Then, at 0929 hours, by which time the British destroyer had approached to 8,000 yards, Z16 opened fire. *Obdurate* retreated, radioing the alarm. Sherbrooke ordered *Obedient* and *Orwell* to concentrate on his flag while *Achates* and the smaller escorts began to lay smoke.

At 0930 the *Lützow* group sighted the British convoy, but Stange, displaying caution above and beyond the call of duty, recalled his destroyers to await better information.

At 0939 *Onslow* followed by *Orwell* was steaming northwest to close both *Obdurate* and the German destroyers when a larger shape hove into view fine on her starboard bow. It was *Hipper*. At 0941 the cruiser opened fire and Sherbrooke broadcast the first definitive enemy report. Burnett received this report, but he kept his cruisers sailing northeast until 0955 to investigate a radar contact which proved to be *Vizalma*. (He believed the convoy was north, not south of his position.)

Onslow and *Orwell* opened fire at *Hipper* from 9,000 yards and played a cat and mouse game for half an hour, simulating torpedo attacks as they dodged in and out of the smoke. As in all Arctic battles the cold played an important role. On *Onslow*, for example, a thin sheet of ice behind the extractors disabled A and X mountings. Ice filmed range finders and binoculars degrading the accuracy of the guns that could fire. *Hipper* initially targeted *Achates* with five salvos. The old destroyer was easily distinguished by a thick, rolling trail of smoke. One seaman recalled: "The enemy picked us out for his early fire. We must have been conspicuous. The German cruiser got us the first time." Actually, a series of very near misses inflicted extensive splinter damage and fractures in her hull plates,

forcing her to reduce speed.

At 0945 hours the convoy turned southeast. At the same time *Hipper* made a sharp alteration to the northeast in response to a feigned torpedo attack. She then returned to her generally easterly course, firing for the next fifteen minutes at the destroyers paralleling her course to the south at ranges between 13,000 to 19,000 yards. By this time Sherbrooke had collected his four O-class vessels, but, uncertain about the location of the German destroyers, he dispatched *Obedient* and *Obdurate* back to the convoy. He did not need to worry. Kummetz was more concerned about *Hipper*'s lines of fire than the potential mayhem his destroyers were capable of inflicting. He kept them on a tight rein behind the cruiser.

Between 1001 and 1016 *Hipper* fired only one salvo. The uncertain visibility whereby sea and cloud merged into a uniform silver-grey affected her aim. With their camouflage, the British ships were hard to see. Kummetz complained: "The light conditions were exceptionally unfavorable, reducing even further the little brightness we could otherwise expect. Everything looked as if covered by a grey veil, which distorted all outlines and merged them together." *Hipper* finally acquired a target at 1016: Sherbrooke's flagship, *Onslow*. Geysers erupted into the sky on either side spraying splinters over her deck and wounding Captain Sherbrooke in the face. Then successive salvos knocked over the destroyer's funnel and aerials and hit her superstructure under B turret and on the forecastle. Severe fires raged throughout *Onslow*'s forward half as she put up a protective smoke screen and turned to starboard.

north of east and was sixteen miles east, northeast of the convoy (sailing southeast at 9 knots). All the destroyers were on the engaged flank between eight and nine miles from the German cruiser. Two of the five were significantly damaged. Meanwhile *Lützow*, trailed by her three destroyers, was a scant five miles south of the convoy which was unwittingly sailing straight toward her. *Sheffield* and *Jamaica* were fifteen miles northwest of *Hipper*. Burnett could see gun flashes to the south, but he adjusted course from a southerly to an easterly heading, wanting to clarify

and came to a parallel course to the north to "wait for the weather to clear." On board *Onslow* the weather was clear enough: "Into view silently slid the huge silhouette of the German pocket battleship. . . . [W]e simply stopped breathing and waited for the first broadside. But nothing happened! As quietly as she came into view she slid out—a ghost ship if ever there was." Raeder wrote: "A favorable opportunity to score a success and possibly finish the appointed job at one blow was not here exploited." Stange had been *Lützow*'s captain for nearly a year, but this was on his first mission and he had never seen action. One can imagine the destruction an aggressive commander, a Philip Vian, even an Alfred Schulze-Hinrichs, would have wrought.

Lützow, taken at sea near the end of 1942. (NHHC)

Sherbrooke remained at his post until his ship was out of danger and then transferred command of the flotilla to Lieutenant Commander D. C. Kinloch of *Obedient*. He received the Victoria Cross for this action. *Hipper* expended forty-eight 8-inch and seventy-two 4.1-inch rounds; she hit the flagship three times in knocking her out of the fight.

At 1030 hours it seemed Kummetz was on the verge of victory. *Hipper* had just altered course to slightly

his radar contacts before he blundered into a surface action.

At 1045 *Rhododendron* reported unidentified ships to the south—they were *Lützow* and her destroyers. Instead of attacking, Stange altered course and passed ahead of the convoy; although his radar was reporting contacts as near as three miles, he couldn't tell what they were because a snow squall providentially (for the British) hid them from his sight. He kept his destroyers astern

At 1030 hours *Bramble* appeared from the northeast. She signaled: "One cruiser bearing 300°." The cruiser was *Hipper* and from 1036 to 1106 she engaged the minesweeper, expending fifty-one 8-inch and thirty-eight 4.1-inch shells, battering the unfortunate ship and leaving her all but sunk. Having run far north, Kummetz detached Z4 and Z16 to finish off the cripple while he hurried south at 31 knots to regain contact. Because the entire German force was now north of the convoy, the escort could concentrate on that side as well, maintaining smoke and standing ready to counter any lunge toward the merchantmen.

At 1115 hours *Achates* had just cleared her own smoke when *Hipper* reappeared to northeast. The cruiser opened fire from 14,000 yards and hit with her first broadside. The 269-pound shell smashed *Achates*' bridge, killing her captain, Lieutenant Commander A. H. T. Johns; other shells struck the destroyer's boiler

All ships required to operate in the Arctic found the weather and sea challenging. Here a German destroyer plunges through heavy seas. (NHHC)

room and forecastle, causing flooding. Her speed fell to 12 knots; forty men died. Nonetheless, she dropped behind the convoy and continued to weave, contributing her only remaining weapon—her black funnel smoke—to the defense. Meanwhile Stange was still waiting. He could see *Hipper*'s gun flashes behind him to the north so at 1126 he came about to the northwest on a reciprocal heading. At the exact same time *Hipper* shifted fire to *Obedient,* flag of Sherbrooke's replacement, Lieutenant Commander Kinloch. The cruiser's gunners continued to shoot effectively, straddling the destroyer from 8,500 yards and destroying her wireless. This forced Kinloch to rotate command to Lieutenant Commander C. E. L. Sclater of *Obdurate.* Regardless of who ordered the defense, however, the tactics remained the same. The destroyers feigned a torpedo attack causing *Hipper* to turn sharply to starboard at 1130.

That same minute *Sheffield* and *Jamaica* finally entered action. Burnett was following his radar, aware he was rapidly closing a contact larger than a destroyer and faster than a merchant ship. Then *Hipper,* heading northeast avoiding imaginary torpedoes, appeared eight miles to the southwest. Burnett turned to a parallel course and at 1131 hours *Sheffield* and then *Jamaica* opened fire. Completely surprised by the columns of water that spouted on either side, *Hipper*'s captain, *Kapitän zur See* Hans Hartmann, ordered a hard 270° turn to starboard. His ship was heeled steeply to port when a 6-inch shell struck her hull eleven feet below the waterline, severely damaging the No. 3 Boiler Room. One thousand tons of water flooded in, knocking No. 2 Boiler Room off line and temporarily reducing speed to 15 knots. At 1135 a second shell struck *Hipper*'s hull amidships on the starboard side and passed through, failing to explode. A third shell detonated in her aircraft hangar igniting a fire. At just that moment Kummetz received a message from the Admiral Polar Seas: "No unnecessary risk." Uncertain about the damage just sustained and the identity of his new opponents, he signaled "Break off, turn away to the west." The time was 1137.

The British cruisers pursued, but *Hipper* vanished into a snow squall. Then, at 1143 *Z16* and *Z4*, trying to find their flag after sinking *Bramble* with all hands, stumbled upon Burnett's cruisers only 4,000 yards to the north. *Sheffield* turned toward *Z16*, the nearer one, and flame erupted from all twelve of her guns. Unaware there were English cruisers in action, Schemmel signaled *Hipper* to stop shooting at him. *Z4*, realizing the awful truth, warned it was the enemy. But it was too late for *Z16*. *Sheffield* hit with her first salvo and badly damaged the destroyer with her third. She checked fire after sixteen broadsides. An observer wrote: "This dark grey wreck of a vessel [passed] down our ship's side. The upper deck short-range weapons raked the burning deck with gun fire as she drifted astern of us into the darkness and oblivion." *Z16* perished with her entire crew of 340 men. *Jamaica* failed to engage *Z4*, which was lucky to escape.

After loitering for more than two hours Stange finally obtained a satisfactorily clear view of the convoy at 1138 as it emerged from the snow squall eight miles to his south. Four minutes later the thunder of *Lützow*'s 11-inch guns finally erupted across the battle sea. She straddled the freighter *Calobre* and splinter damage forced the merchant ship to drop out of line. Sclater responded by leading his destroyers to the threatened flank, laying heavy smoke while the convoy made an emergency turn to starboard. Stange continued to the northwest, fighting a leisurely battle, periodically engaging targets with his main and secondary batteries. (His ship only expended eighty-six 11-inch and seventy-six 5.9-inch rounds the entire battle).

Following behind Z6 and Z30 managed to snap off a few rounds and some torpedoes as well (the frustration of the destroyer captains can be imagined) but the Germans did no further harm except for severe splinter damage *Lützow* inflicted on *Obdurate* at 1200 hours (which required five weeks in dock to repair). When *Hipper* briefly appeared to the west of *Lützow* Sclater [of *Obdurate*] turned toward her and came under fire, but at 1149 Kummetz ordered the fleet to withdraw. Dark was drawing near and his orders forbade night combat. At 1203 Stange received this order and immediately complied.

At 1230 there was a brief engagement between the British and German cruisers. The shooting of both forces was good with *Lützow* straddling Burnett's ships and being straddled in turn. But neither side appeared to have the heart for a slugfest and Burnett (wisely) altered course to the northwest at 1236. *Achates* finally capsized and sank at 0115 hours.

That a German "pocket battleship," heavy cruiser and five destroyers would flee from a pair of British light cruisers was a powerful statement of how the nature of the surface war had changed since December 1939 and the Battle of the River Plate. In fact, the Battle of the Barents Sea was one of the most decisive naval battles of World War II because of the impact it had on the future use of the German navy's large warships. Berlin expected success and the initial reports only heightened that anticipation. Then Führer headquarters heard nothing until the BBC announced a great victory. The consequences of Hitler's disappointment led to the downfall of *Grossadmiral* Raeder and an order to pay off every surface warship larger than a destroyer. While this order was never carried out as originally delivered, it nonetheless gutted the surface fleet as a fighting force. Before Barents Sea the German Navy fought twenty-nine surface actions and nine involved cruisers or larger ships. After Barents Sea the navy fought thirty-seven actions and only one involved a heavy unit.

The light cruiser *Sheffield*. Her battery of a dozen 6-inch guns annihilated the destroyer *Z16*, which sank with the loss of her crew of 340 men. *Sheffield* and *Jamaica*, which the month before had been trading salvoes with French destroyers in the Mediterranean, managed to discourage the much more heavily armed German ships from pursuing the convoy. (NHHC)

BOMBARDMENTS AND ACTIONS IN THE BALTIC SEA FROM JANUARY 1944 TO WAR'S END

By July 1944 Soviet surface forces were operating openly in the Baltic for the first time since the fall of 1941. Here a column of Russian patrol boats sails close inshore. (NHHC)

From the fall of 1941 to the beginning of 1944 the Soviet Union's Baltic shoreline consisted of a tiny enclave around Leningrad and a few small islands in the Gulf of Finland. Massive mine barriers in the gulf bottled up the Soviet fleet, keeping this great inland sea a haven for German forces. Vital supplies from Sweden could be shipped to the Reich, and surface and submarine forces could train in tranquility, a condition *Prinz Eugen* enjoyed as she spent the summer and fall of 1943 training naval cadets.

The Baltic situation started to change in January 1944, when a Soviet offensive finally pushed the Germans away from Leningrad and moved the front line west to the old Estonian/Soviet border. Nevertheless, the Soviet fleet (which consisted of one battleship, two cruisers, two flotilla leaders, eight destroyers, twenty-eight submarines, and nearly four hundred smaller vessels) remained confined to the eastern part of the Gulf of Finland. On 5 January *Prinz Eugen* had another change of command as *Kapitän zur See* Hans-Jürgen Reinicke replaced Captain Erhardt. Reinicke had previously been Admiral Ciliax's chief of staff and participated in the Channel Dash in that role. His appointment marked the return of *Prinz Eugen* to active service.

On 13 February Hitler asked Dönitz whether the navy could support the army's battle in Estonia. The next day the admiral formed *Prinz Eugen*, *Admiral Scheer*, two destroyers, and six torpedo boats into an operational unit—called the 2nd Task Force—to be used to support the army upon request. The cruiser did not get back into the war on this occasion, however, as the new front east of Estonia held and the imperative for naval intervention faded.

Prinz Eugen's first war mission since her aborted January 1943 attempts to reach Norway came on 19 June 1944, when, flying the flag of *Vizeadmiral* August Thiele, she slipped from Gotenhafen and headed for the Gulf of Finland to support Finnish troops under heavy pressure from Soviet forces driving north from Leningrad. She sailed with *T10*, *T11*, and *F10* to the area south of the Åland Islands. First *Z25* and *Z35* joined *Prinz Eugen* and then on 25th *Lützow*, *T3*, *T4*, *T12*, and *Z28*. The Soviets had conducted several small amphibious landings, and the naval force was there to ensure these operations did not become more ambitious. The ships were also to serve as visible signs of German support and—in the case of a sudden Finnish collapse— to carry forces that could quickly occupy the islands.

THE BALTIC

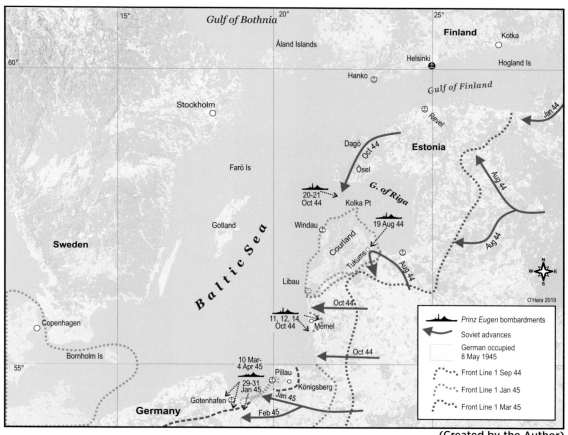

(Created by the Author)

On the 27th, after it appeared the crisis was passing, *Prinz Eugen* returned to Gotenhafen.

The event that completely ruptured the German position in Russia was Operation Bagration, the Soviet summer 1944 offensive against the German Army Group Center. This presented the German navy with a host of tasks and challenges that persisted for the remainder of the war. In brief, these consisted of:

1. Escorting traffic and supplying by sea huge pockets of territory cut off by the Soviet advance

2. Supporting the ground troops directly with bombardments or indirectly by establishing a naval presence in contested waters

3. Evacuating troops and civilians from threatened locations

The destruction of Army Group Center in July forced German troops to begin withdrawing from Estonia. More dangerous, from the German point of view, was a Soviet thrust into Latvia that threatened to cut off Army Group North. On 1 August the Soviets captured Tukums, west of Riga, isolating large numbers of German troops still in northern Latvia and Estonia. To support counterattacking forces that were trying to reestablish communications, *Prinz Eugen* sailed from Gotenhafen on 19 August escorted by *T23* and *T28*. That night she rounded Kolka Point and entered the Gulf of Riga, meeting along the way *Z25*, *Z28*, *Z35*, and *Z36*. Sailing stealthily with all lights extinguished, and unsure if they would encounter mines or submarines,

the ships of the German squadron neared the end of the strategic body of water that had seen such intense naval combat in World War I. First the cruiser launched all three of her Arado aircraft.

Next, at 0802, *Prinz Eugen*'s main battery opened fire. Her aircraft dropped bombs and reported on the accuracy of the gunfire. Her initial target was the railroad station at Tukums; she then engaged a second target in the town and finally a Soviet artillery battery north of it. The cruiser expended 265 20.3-cm rounds in observed fire. One account credited the cruiser with smashing forty-eight T34 tanks "as they paraded in the town hall square in Tukums prior to a Soviet attack." The destroyers also bombarded targets along the coast. The army considered the results good.

The counterattack reestablished communications with Riga, and the Germans were able to hold the city for another two months. Meanwhile, the cruiser's crew could take satisfaction in having conducted a successful war mission; the morale benefits of firing the big guns at the enemy were considerable.

As the German armies withdrew west, continued pressure on Finland caused that county to seek a cease-fire with the Soviet Union, which went into effect on 4 September. The German navy was concerned that with the northern coast of the Gulf of Finland no longer under Axis control, the Soviet navy would win unimpeded access to the Baltic. In an ill-advised attempt to keep the Soviets bottled up, the Germans attempted to seize Finnish-occupied Hogland Island in the middle of the Gulf of Finland. This was called Operation *Tanne Ost*. There was also a sister operation called *Tanne West* to capture the Åland lands at the entrance to the Gulf of Bothnia, but command canceled this operation on the 4th. The Germans believed that their former Finnish allies would, at worst, offer token resistance. *Prinz*

An Arado aircraft mounted on the catapult and ready for launch, as soon as the pilot climbs into the cockpit. These aircraft were slow but very maneuverable. In the Tukums action three planes spotted, dropped bombs, and even sparred with Soviet fighters. All returned with light damage. (U.S. Naval Institute photo archive)

The floatplane generally landed in a calmed area in the cruiser's lee and was then hoisted on board with the ship's crane. (U.S. Naval Institute photo archive)

operation's complete failure. *Prinz Eugen* was back in Gotenhafen by the 18th.

The cruiser's time in port was brief; she weighed again on the 21th, this time bound for the Gulf of Bothnia, where a German convoy of a tanker, six merchant vessels, and three motorized barges were sailing south from the ex-German base at Kemi at the head of the gulf. *Prinz Eugen*, *Lützow*, four destroyers, and three torpedo boats waited south of the Åland Islands in case Finnish coastal batteries tried to interfere with the passage of the German vessels. The Finns, however, had no desire to escalate hostilities with Germany and let the convoy pass. The 2nd Task Force was back in Gotenhafen by 25 September.

The Germans' situation continued to deteriorate as Soviet forces relentlessly pressed forward. Estonia was back in Soviet hands by the beginning of October. The German navy was anxious to collaborate with the army and was even ready to risk the heavy ships in narrow waters should such actions "serve the attainment of

Eugen and five torpedo boats were put at the disposal of Admiral Eastern Baltic to support the operation if needed. The heavy cruiser departed Gotenhafen on 13 September. The landing force of 1,545 men established several toeholds on the narrow and rocky island, but the Finnish defenders resisted energetically, easily containing these while Soviet aircraft hindered German efforts to reinforce and supply the landings. Command considered conditions too dangerous for *Prinz Eugen* to venture into the gulf. She waited two hundred miles to the west, experiencing scattered and ineffectual air attacks while the Finns slaughtered the German landing force. The end results were 1,300 casualties and the

Prinz Eugen's main battery in action against Soviet land targets. She had last fired her 20.3-cm battery in earnest two and a half years before against British destroyers in the North Sea. All accounts agree that her crew was happy to participate once again in the war effort. (Koop and Schmolke)

The armored ship (redesignated as a heavy cruiser) *Lützow* in late 1944. She served alongside *Prinz Eugen* in the 2nd Task Force in the Baltic in late 1944 and early 1945. (Koop and Schmolke)

important operational aims, such as supporting a major military campaign or assisting the Army in a difficult disengaging movement or withdrawal from the enemy." It also felt that the use of the heavy ships would send an important political message to Sweden. To this end the 2nd Task Force—*Prinz Eugen, Lützow,* and the 6th Destroyer Flotilla—was kept at three hours' notice at Gotenhafen. By early October Soviet spearheads were approaching the Baltic coast in the vicinity of Memel, a Lithuanian port that had been annexed by Germany in 1939, and the task force went into action. From 11 October through the afternoon of the 12th *Prinz Eugen* fired 673 rounds at twenty distinct targets in the Memel area at ranges that varied from fifteen to thirty thousand meters. At 1100 on the 12th, five Soviet torpedo bombers ineffectually attacked the cruiser but afterward caused some casualties in strafing runs. She claimed one aircraft shot down. *Lützow* contributed 400 28.3-cm and 245 15-cm shells and the destroyers Z25 and Z35 a hundred rounds each. This was the longest sustained action the cruiser's guns had ever undertaken, and the ship suffered considerable shock damage. The Grossdeutschland Division, which was defending the city, sent a message of thanks indicating the bombardment had had a positive impact. The naval war diary noted: "The 12th October was a calm day at

The *Durchhalt* Strategy

EXTRACTED FROM *HITLER, DÖNITZ, AND THE BALTIC SEA: THE THIRD REICH'S LAST HOPE, 1944–1945* BY HOWARD D. GRIER, NAVAL INSTITUTE PRESS

Hitler's strategy in 1944 and 1945 has been referred to as the *Durchhalt* strategy, holding out at all costs. Although many former German generals claim it consisted of nothing more than clinging tenaciously to every foot of ground and hoping for the best, it was actually a broad strategy with military, political, and economic aspects. Hitler's first concern was to retain the areas economically essential to continue the war. Speer's August 1944 study of

raw materials helped him determine some of the boundaries of the reduced Reich. The Wehrmacht's dependence on oil required the inclusion of Hungary, and this explains why in January 1945, after the Ardennes Offensive failed, Hitler shifted troops from the West to Hungary rather than to East Prussia or Poland. Dönitz's demands to defend the shores of the eastern Baltic and Norway for the new U-boat offensive meant that Hitler had to hang on to those areas as well.

With raw materials and strategically vital geographic regions in German hands, Hitler would concentrate on the other military and political aspects of the *Durchhalt* strategy. . . . Along with jet aircraft and unmanned rockets, which are better known, the Type XXI U-boats represented one of the miracle weapons integral to the *Durchhalt* strategy. From mid-1943 on Dönitz advocated the defense of every foot of ground, especially in the East, to buy time for the new U-boat force.

the front of Memel; this is assumed to be attributable to the gunfire from the sea." Also, "The operation was extremely valuable for the increase of the fighting strength of the task force. The morale and attitude of the crews were excellent."

On the 14th, after refueling and reprovisioning, *Prinz Eugen*, supported by *Z35*, *T9*, *T13*, and *T21*, was back in action. On the 14th she expended 246 rounds beginning at 0930. *Lützow* joined her after 1500. The cruiser fired another 368 rounds on the 15th on a total of eighteen different targets. She claimed 84 percent of her observed fire was on target. These actions exhausted Gotenhafen's supply of 20.3-cm ammunition, forcing

the navy to ship in more. The Germans noted from Soviet radio traffic that the shore bombardments were generating complaints from local commanders to their superiors and that a much stronger aerial counterattack should be expected.

As it turned out, the shell shortage did not affect the heavy cruiser's operations. *Prinz Eugen* was returning to Gotenhafen on the 15th, sailing through very thick fog, when, at 2200, she encountered the light cruiser *Leipzig* lying directly across her path. *Leipzig* had stopped and was in the process of uncoupling her diesels and connecting the turbines. Because of the danger from Soviet submarines, neither cruiser was showing any lights, and *Leipzig* had inadvertently drifted into the shipping lane.

Reportedly two of the light cruiser's carpenters were playing chess in their workshop, located between the bridge and funnel on an upper deck. Suddenly the bulkhead split open: *Prinz Eugen*'s bow appeared, separated the two men, and knocked over the

Dönitz was determined to do his part to make sure the navy did not falter. Thus,

an analysis of German strategy on land and at sea in the final eighteen months of World War II brings to light the decisive importance of the Baltic theater. When the Soviets began to force Army Group North back from Leningrad in January 1944, Hitler repeatedly insisted upon the defense of coastal sectors, first along the Gulf of Finland and then on the Baltic. By forbidding a retreat from the Narva area

he permitted the Soviets temporarily to isolate the army group in Estonia and eastern Latvia in the summer of 1944. Hitler's refusal to withdraw . . . forces from the Riga area then enabled the Russians again to sever the army group's land contact with the Reich, this time for good, through their attack to the coast near Memel at the beginning of October. This process of isolation was later repeated with Army Group Center/North and Army Group Vistula in East and West Prussia. Of all the bridgeheads

German troops defended along the Baltic in the final seven months of the war, only those in Courland, on the Hela Peninsula, and at the mouth of Vistula River held out until Germany's surrender. Over one million German soldiers fought in the Baltic bridgeheads, and most of these troops therefore could not participate in the defense of areas previously considered to be the most decisive to Nazi Germany's survival, namely the Ruhr and Silesian industrial areas, and the Reich capital, Berlin.

On 15 October 1944 *Prinz Eugen* rammed *Leipzig* outside Gotenhafen. The light cruiser was at sea to lay mines and was dead in the water at the time, switching her propulsion from diesel to turbines. The two ships were locked together for sixteen hours before *Prinz Eugen* managed to back free. This photo shows the moment the cruisers separated. Beyond *Leipzig* a tug can be seen holding the light cruiser stationary. (U.S. Naval Institute photo archive)

This photo shows *Prinz Eugen*'s damaged stem. She was in dock two weeks repairing the damage. (U.S. Naval Institute photo archive)

UNITED STATES NAVAL INSTITUTE

During her bombardment of the Sworbe Peninsula, *Prinz Eugen* came under fire from Soviet shore batteries. This photo shows the cruiser withdrawing from danger as a torpedo boat makes smoke in her wake. (Koop and Schmolk)

chessboard. The heavy cruiser cut the smaller ship nearly in half. The two ships were locked together until 1430 the next day, when *Prinz Eugen* finally succeeded in backing clear. Her damage was characterized as "not important," but she needed to dock to repair her bow. She was taken in hand at Deutsche Werke Gotenhafen. The repair was made a top priority, and *Prinz Eugen* was out of dockyard hands on 7 November.

Prinz Eugen undertook her next war mission on 19 November. Germans on Ösel Island were desperately holding on to the Sworbe Peninsula, preserving access into the Gulf of Riga from the west for the Germans and denying it to the Soviets. The Germans wanted to hold the position as long as possible so they could operate on the east side of the bridgehead on the Courland Peninsula and deny the Soviets the use of Riga. The cruiser sailed under the escort of *T13, T19, T16,* and *T21.* Soon *Z35, Z36,* and *Z43* joined. The weather was stormy, with winds blowing Force 6–7 and visibility only a few thousand yards. It was not until 1405 on the 20th that the cruiser was able to open fire, expending 255 rounds. Observers ashore reported accurate gunfire; enemy shore batteries that fired back were well off target.

That night the German warships withdrew west to the vicinity of Gotland before returning the next day. On the 21st *Prinz Eugen* expended 259 rounds in a shoot that began at 1048 and lasted until 1540. Over

the two days she had engaged a dozen targets and fired 198 10.5-cm rounds. All fire was unobserved. Using up her allotment of ammunition, the cruiser stood off and handed shore bombardment duties over to *Admiral Scheer.*

After so much action the cruiser's gun barrels needed to be relined, and so she returned to dock at the beginning of December for this work and to have her antiaircraft suite enhanced. Conditions were chaotic, and even the supply of electricity was periodic. The work took five weeks, and the ship did not emerge from the shipyard until January. By this time the front lines were on German soil. Not only 20.3-cm ammunition was in short supply but also fuel and even food. Refugees were pouring west. The Germans had suffered 840,000 killed or missing on the eastern front since the start of Operation Bagration and nearly half that many on the western front. Finland, Bulgaria, and Romania had changed sides, and even Sweden had stopped shipping iron ore to Germany. Warsaw was in revolt, and the lower Balkans had been evacuated. It seemed clear that the war was nearing its end—clear, at least to everyone except the German high command, which continued to believe that miracle weapons such as new submarines and rockets could change the tide of battle.

When *Prinz Eugen* was once again ready for sea, Gotenhafen and Königsberg had been cut off by land, and Memel had fallen. The town's garrison

Lützow and *Scheer* took over on the bombardment line.

From 10 March through 4 April 1945 *Prinz Eugen* was active in the Danzig Bight. She fired 2,025 20.3-cm rounds, 99 of which were observed, on 132 different targets, claiming 81 percent of rounds on target. She also fired 2,025 20.3-cm rounds on 132 different targets, 99 of which were observed, claiming 81 percent for the 739 that had been observed. On one occasion the *Prinz Eugen*'s artillery liaison officer, flown to the forward German line, requested fire on four approaching Russian tanks. The range was found to be 13 miles. After the first salvo from the cruiser he reported: "Two tanks hit and on fire."

Gotenhafen fell on 28 March, and from this point the priority was to evacuate as many refugees as possible; *Prinz Eugen* concentrated on escorting the refugee convoys. She was hit on 31 March by rockets that killed nine men, but in general Soviet submarines, warships, and aircraft affected her activities remarkably little. The ship shot off her last forty 20.3-cm shells on 4 April, and then, unable to participate any longer in combat, she sailed west, arriving in Copenhagen on the 20th of April. She was there when the war came to an end.

was withdrawing south along the spit of land that separated the Baltic from the Kurisches Haff, hoping for evacuation by sea. On 26 January 1945 *Prinz Eugen* replenished with fuel and ammunition in Gotenhafen and then, at 0000 on the 29th, with *Z25*, *T23*, and *T33*, she set forth on an eight-hour voyage to the firing line. Starting at 0850 she engaged several targets. At 1850 she withdrew for the night to Hela but was back at 0755 the next morning, firing until poor visibility that afternoon forced a stop. Over the two days she pounded thirty-five different targets in unobserved fire, expending 871 shells. After another night in Hela, *Prinz Eugen* continued her bombardment, but by this time 20.3-cm ammunition was nearly expended;

Although the Soviet Baltic Fleet had a battleship, cruisers, and destroyers, it never ventured out to take on the German 2nd Task Force. Aircraft, submarines, and smaller craft likewise did little to bother the German cruisers and destroyers. This photo shows a *Moskva*-class gunboat armed with 76-mm tank turrets. This is representative of the type of vessel the Soviets used to support their land forces in coastal waters. (NHHC)

UNDER TWO FLAGS

USS *PRINZ EUGEN* (IX 300), THE ATOMIC BOMB TESTS AT BIKINI ATOLL, AND AFTER

Prinz Eugen at Copenhagen, Denmark, in May 1945. (U.S. Naval Institute photo archive)

From Kiel to Kwajalein

EXTRACTED FROM "HISTORIC SHIPS" BY J. M. CAIELLA, *NAVAL HISTORY*, AUGUST 2017

Included among the most unusual ships ever to serve with the U.S. Navy was perhaps its most unwanted—the German World War II heavy cruiser *Prinz Eugen* (IX-300). By the end of the conflict, the cruiser was the Kriegsmarine's largest, most modern, and most famous remaining warship.

After arriving in Copenhagen on 20 April 1945, the cruiser essentially was demilitarized when she debunkered her fuel for transfer to destroyers, which could transport troops more efficiently. With their fight over, the crew, under command of Captain Hans-Jürgen Reinicke, maintained their ship as they awaited her uncertain fate. At 1600 on 7

May, with the crew assembled on the quarterdeck, per orders from the new President of Germany, Grand Admiral Karl Dönitz, the national ensign was taken down and replaced by the international white flag of surrender.

The British officially took the cruiser on 22 May, with Captain Robert F. Elkins of the light cruiser HMS *Dido* assuming command. In his brief inspection of the ship, Elkins found a number of innovations that would be of interest to other navies, not the least of which was her boiler construction, which allowed the ship to go from cold [iron] to seaworthy in only 45 minutes. These innovations combined with the fact that she

was the last major German warship constructed with the most recent improvements, made the *Prinz Eugen* valuable to the victors.

Two days later, in consort with the only other remaining Kriegsmarine capital ship, the light cruiser *Nürnberg,* the heavy cruiser began a three-day trip ostensibly to a more secure port, Wilhelmshaven, Germany, but in reality the British hoped to prevent the ship from being scuttled.

During the Potsdam Conference (17 July–2 August 1945), Allied leaders discussed the aftermath of Germany's defeat and the further conduct of the Pacific war; division of Kriegsmarine assets was a minor concern. The parties earlier had decided they would divide the remains equally based on the decision of a Tripartite Naval Commission, consisting of representatives from each of the three major Allied powers. The commission would discuss only surface units; each government would receive ten U-boats, and the remaining submarines would be destroyed. Deadline for completion

(above) Offloading ammunition at Copenhagen. (U.S. Naval Institute photo archive)

(right) Transferring the ship to British command. (U.S. Naval Institute photo archive)

Nürnberg under way from Copenhagen to Wilhelmshaven. A pair of B-24s are overtaking her at low attitude. (Canadian DND)

of all transfers was set for 18 February 1946.

By agreement, vice admirals headed each delegation; however, the Soviets promoted their representative to admiral the weekend before the commission convened in Berlin on 14 August. U.S. representative Vice Admiral Robert L. Ghormley was amused but did not relinquish the chairman's gavel.

A subcommittee drew up a list of German ships for division—with the Russians arguing for inclusion of racing sculls. Virtually every discussion involved the *Prinz Eugen* and her future. Despite some interesting features, the United States saw little value in the ship and had no vested interest in obtaining her other than to prevent the Soviets from gaining the most significant naval prize. In the end, the commission agreed on 19 October to divide the ships among three lists: A—the *Prinz*

Eugen and seven destroyers; B—the *Nürnberg* and nine destroyers; and C—13 destroyers. The next roadblock was to determine package distribution. After much wrangling, U.S. Navy Captain Arthur H. Graubart suggested drawing lots, which was quickly accepted. He wrote the letters on note cards, placed them in his hat, and held it over his head. The Soviets drew first; it was B. The British next drew C, leaving Vice Admiral Ghormley to draw A and the *Prinz Eugen*.

The cruiser, then in dry dock, transferred to U.S. control on 16 December, and at the end of the month, Captain Graubart took command. At 1000 on 5 January 1946, the *Prinz Eugen* officially joined the U.S. Navy when Graubart put the ship "in American service" as IX-300. The transfer was not the smoothest. Graubart told Captain Reinicke, who was still on board, that he would

issue the orders putting the ship in service to both the U.S. crew and the German crew. Reinicke argued that he was captain of the cruiser and would relay the orders. Graubart replied that his counterpart was ex-captain of the *Prinz Eugen* and that he, Graubart, was captain of the USS *Prinz Eugen* (IX-300). Reinicke could not argue the point.

On 13 January the cruiser departed her homeland for the last time, manned by 600 Germans and 88 Americans. Ten days later she arrived in Boston Harbor. There both crews learned that the ship would be used for conventional testing and then Operations Crossroads nuclear-bomb testing in the Pacific, to be followed by her later destruction. In early February, the *Prinz Eugen* moved to Philadelphia Navy Yard. There she was thoroughly inspected and certain equipment was removed for detailed testing. The two A turret

Prinz Engen under way from Copenhagen to Wilhelmshaven. A British destroyer is escorting. A B-24 is flying very low on the ship's starboard side aft. (Canadian DND)

8-inch guns were removed, along with gunnery optics, antiaircraft towers and controls, and the aircraft catapult and its accompanying two Arado Ar 196 A-5 seaplanes.

Her trip to Bikini Atoll began on 11 March. En route the cruiser stopped in San Diego, California, for repairs and removal of her sonar gear. After additional testing, the German crew was released from duty on 1 May. Reinicke secretively weighted down the ship's naval ensign that had been lowered during her surrender in Copenhagen and dropped it into the Pacific. Transit to Pearl Harbor took nine days from her departure on 10 May. The cruiser's boilers had broken down, and she needed to be towed into port. Her final transit began on 3 June and ended six days later with her arrival at Bikini.

Situated approximately 1,200 yards from the detonation point on Able Day, 1 July, when a Fat Man bomb as used on Nagasaki was air dropped, the *Prinz Eugen* received only superficial damage and minimal radiation contamination. She was less fortunate on 25 July, Baker Day, when a similar weapon was detonated while suspended 90 feet below the landing ship LSM-60. Anchored farther away from the blast point at 2,000 yards, the cruiser suffered slight damage with minor flooding in both steering and engineering compartments. But it was fatal. Contamination was considered lethal, thus repairs could not be made.

Late that month the *Prinz Eugen* was moved to Kwajalein Lagoon—formerly German territory—where she sank on 22 December. A propeller was recovered and donated by the Navy to Germany for a naval memorial in Kiel. What remains of the wreck is significantly deteriorated.

(top left) *Prinz Eugen* looking aft from the forecastle, showing 20.3-cm guns, bridge, and main-battery fire control. Taken while ship was in a floating drydock, at Wilhelmshaven, soon after V-E Day. (NHHC)

(top right) *Prinz Eugen* on 15 March 1946 passing through the Panama Canal. (NHHC)

(bottom right) *Prinz Eugen* (IX 300) passing through the Gatun Locks, Panama Canal. The guns have been removed from A turret. (NHHC)

The atomic bomb tests at Bikini seem like atrocities against nature from today's perspective. At the time, however, little was known of the effects and consequences of such testing. Rear Admiral Robert Conard participated in Operation Crossroads and recorded his memories in 1993.

The Bikini test proved to be one of the most challenging events of my career. There were a tremendous number of ships involved and thousands of personnel. We were testing the effects of the atomic bomb on Navy ships. At that time,

the effects of atomic weapons was [sic] practically unknown, and so this was a new field we were getting into. Following training of 4 or 5 months in different AEC laboratories I went to Bikini as a radiological safety officer. I was on a patrol boat that went in after the first atom bomb test. This first explosion was an awesome sight, the first of many I would later see. I was on a ship. And then the ship came and let us off into the water just outside of Bikini. I had eight men with me on our patrol boat, and we steamed into the lagoon, and with some trepidation, because we really

didn't know what we were going to face. The effect of the bomb was obvious as some of the ships were damaged and smoking. But fortunately, this was an airburst with no fallout and there was little radiation involvement. We were able to clear the ships for boarding soon. But the second test, the bigger test, was an underwater test, and that proved to have a much more serious aftereffect, because the radioactive material was mixed with the water and the ships were contaminated. It was a much more difficult operation. I was on one of the ships that had to do with recovering the technological instruments, clearing personnel, and being sure they were showered and properly decontaminated. So this was quite an experience for me.

(top) *Prinz Eugen* is to the right during the Baker test. (AP)

(bottom) Bikini Atoll, 25 July 1946, *Prinz Eugen* is behind the blast, left center. (U.S. Naval Institute photo archive)

Following the Bikini operation, target ships were towed down to Kwajalein and I was ordered there to check the ships as they came in and removed ammunition. So we had our men wear respirators since we were afraid that plutonium and other fission products might be present on the ships. That proved to be a very tricky operation, with the difficulties of going down in a hot ship and bringing back all the ammunition. Some of the target ships were more damaged than others. I remember one of the ships, the *Prinz Eugen*. It was a beautiful German cruiser, and when it was towed into Kwajalein we went on board. I couldn't help but admire the beauty of the ship. Inside was all the silverware, all the fine furniture. Everything was left intact, and it was in pretty good shape, we thought. And then about a week later, we got word that she was sinking. Apparently, one of the seams in the ship had been loosened by the atomic blast. I went on board when she was beginning to go down. We got off in time, but she went on under and even to this day, in the lagoon, the stern of that ship can be seen just above the water level.

Baker Day atomic bomb test, 25 July, fifteen seconds after detonation. Identifiable ships left to right are *Pennsylvania, New York, Salt Lake City, Nagato*, and *Nevada. Prinz Eugen* is off the frame to the right. (NHHC)

The End of the *Prinz*

BY CAPTAIN GEORGE L. DICKEY JR., *PROCEEDINGS*, AUGUST 1969

The scene now shifts to Bikini Atoll, Marshall Islands, in the spring of 1946. The United States had used nuclear fission weapons in war, but wished to find out much more about the power and varied effects unleashed by this new weapon. Consequently, the Navy had gathered a large fleet of ships for Operation Crossroads, two separate tests of atomic bombs. The target fleet consisted mainly of an assortment of U.S. Navy ships—old battleships, two carriers, some old cruisers and destroyers, submarines, and troop transports, plus various smaller surface units. The *Prinz Eugen*, now dubbed *IX-300*, and two ex-Japanese ships, the battleship *Nagato* and the cruiser *Sakawa*, completed the target array. Another sizeable contingent of ships provided command and support functions.

The *Prinz Eugen* was not especially close to either bomb burst, and no particularly significant damage was recorded as a result of the first test—an air burst. Like most of the targets, the *Prinz Eugen* received radioactive contamination from the underwater burst a few days later. When radiation intensities permitted an inspection, water was discovered in one of the machinery spaces, but no damage was found, and no further flooding noted. It was assumed that a leaky valve was the cause.

Subsequently, the remaining ships were towed to Kwajalein and anchored in the lagoon while the U. S. authorities tried to figure out what to do with these 50 or so contaminated ships. The Navy decontaminated a few for experimental purposes, but most were too old, tired, and battle-worn to be economically returned to duty, even if they had been needed.

A main military air route passed through Kwajalein in those days, and passengers on the planes saw from the air what looked like a formidable fleet anchored in the lagoon. It was, however, a dead fleet; nevertheless, there was a lot of activity. A large working party scattered to the ships each day to offload the many tons of live ammunition for jettisoning in deep water. An inspection and salvage team inspected each ship daily to detect signs of flooding or damage. Each party boarding a contaminated ship passed through a "change station," where the men donned special clothing and obtained the oxygen breathing apparatus and cannisters required to be

worn by persons below decks. At least one radiological safety officer accompanied each boarding detail. At noon, all hands were sent to the decontamination station to clean up, change, and be monitored with Geiger counters to ensure that all contamination was washed off. This set of procedures was repeated for every boarding, and it remains essentially the same today for similar activity.

The *Prinz Eugen* remained sleek and beautiful among such old-timers as the battleships *Pennsylvania* and *Nevada*, the heavily damaged light carrier *Independence*, and the old cruisers *Salt Lake City* and *Pensacola*. Unfortunately, demise was just as inglorious as her attempts at wartime success.

Between 0700 and 1030 on 21 December 1946 she took on a noticeable list and was down by the stern. The meager forces on Kwajalein rushed to attempt salvage. Normally, the mainstay of the salvage organization was USS *Conserver* (ARS-30), but early that morning she had departed Kwajalein to a ship in distress some distance away.

She took with her the know-how, towing horsepower, and salvage equipment counted [on] to form the basis of any salvage operation. Commodore George A. Seitz, U. S. Navy, Atoll Commander and himself an aviator, looked over his resources with dismay. He had two small tugs and two LCIs which quickly took aboard extra shore-based pumps. His assistants did not exemplify a wealth of talent: an aviator lieutenant who was assistant port director (the port director was detached before his relief arrived), and two ensigns, all quite deficient in experience and knowledge for the task at hand.

A below-decks inspection of the ship revealed extensive flooding. The party did not go below the third deck, for the watertight boundaries to lower decks seemed secure and here was some fear of the radioactive contamination. The major flooding was below this level, but the list of the ship had placed the lower row of ports at the water's surface, Many of these were badly sprung, with openings of an inch or more even when dogged, which permitted considerable water to build up on the third deck level. The pump capacity was unequal to the task, and the list continued to increase. Seitz realized that the *Prinz Eugen* must be beached to prevent blocking the harbor. Beaching plans had been worked out well before this first test, but the designated beaching area was directly upwind

Prinz Eugen capsized on the reef at Enubuj, Kwajalein Atoll. (U.S. Naval Institute photo archive)

of the ship on this day, and a brisk breeze had sprung up. The Commodore had insufficient tug power available to buck the wind, so he dispatched one of the inexperienced ensigns (the author) for a hasty survey of downwind Enubuj Island, the next most likely spot. A new plan quickly followed, and the two little tugs took the *Prinz Eugen* in tow.

Seitz wanted to put her stern into the wind en route, aim her bow at the island, and use the combined power of wind and tugs to ram her bow onto the coral shelf which lay some 30 feet deep and a few dozen yards offshore. All went well at first. The tugs hauled the ship around, but as the final run began, the wind took over and pushed her around broadside to wind and island. The tugs were completely helpless. For the last few hundred yards, the *Prinz Eugen* drifted rather slowly onto the ledge, her port side to the island. The time was 1900. Another try was futile; the tugs could not budge her.

During the night the list increased to over 35 degrees. At 1243 on 22 December, the *Prinz Eugen* rolled over slowly and turned bottom up. Radiological safety teams monitored the area and gathered loose, contaminated debris to rule out any hazard to personnel. Some months later, divers inspected most of the underwater body and found no apparent damage. The official follow-up report hypothesized that a large sea valve must have carried away to have caused such fast flooding. It further stated that dislodging the hulk and towing it to deep water was quite infeasible. In later years, commercial companies inquired about salvaging the *Prinz Eugen* for scrap. Each time, memories of the original radiological hazard have dictated a negative reply.

Though she had participated in two memorable operations, the *Prinz Eugen*'s contributions to Germany's naval war effort were minimal; a great deal of her time had been spent undergoing assorted repairs or remaining inactive. In the end, she was the first relatively undamaged ship in the Bikini target array to give up and sink; her comparatively ancient and harder-used sister target ships rode at anchor for months before being forcibly disposed of at sea.

For some mysterious reason, Lady Luck had never deigned to smile on Germany's *Prinz Eugen*. The battle success that might-have-been hers remained always out of reach and somehow glory passed her by.

Pieces of *Prinz Eugen* survived the ship. The sound gear and other electronics were removed when she passed through San Diego on her way to Honolulu. In mid-1948 the Naval Electronics Laboratory installed these and other electronics on board USS *Witek* (DD 848) in place of a twin 5-inch mount. The destroyer tested this equipment for two years until it was eventually removed at Norfolk in 1950. One of her aircraft (T3 + BH) is in a storage facility of the Smithsonian. Her bell is at the U.S. Naval Museum in Washington and the guns of A turret are at the testing facility in Dahgren, Virginia. In 1978, of one of her propellers was removed from the wreck and is on display at the Laboe Naval Memorial near Kiel.

Prior to the atomic bomb tests *Prinz Eugen* was loaded with approximately 2,700 tons of oil so that the test conditions would be as realistic as possible. She retained this load when she capsized. A 1974 U.S. Navy report recommended that the oil be removed within thirty years. In 1986 the U.S. government transferred ownership of the wreck to the Republic of the Marshall Islands. The wreck shifted in 1989 and it appeared further shifting was likely due to superstructure corrosion and collapse. The coral reef the wreck sits upon was also probably degrading. In 2010 the Marshall Islands asked the United States for technical and financial assistance in removing oil from the wreck's bunkers. Initially the United States responded that it was the responsibility of the Marshall Islands to pay for any such work. However, the U.S. Fish and Wildlife Service assessed the risk of a catastrophic oil spill as high and estimated in 2014 that the cost of oil removal could range up to $20 million. The U.S. Navy began examining the problem in 2016 and in 2018 the U.S. Congress made Army funds available to recover the oil. Planning to accomplish this task began in February 2018 with the deployment of a site survey team which examined the wreck, anchoring sites, and the best ways to extract, transfer, and enclose the oil.

On 1 September 2018, a team of divers from Mobile Diving Salvage Unit operating from the rescue and salvage ship USNS *Salvor* (T-ARS 52) and supported by the commercial tanker *Humber* began the task. The first stage involved the placement of nine mooring anchors to hold both vessels over the wreck. Once the ships were in place the divers began drilling holes in the hull at the highest location of each of the exterior tanks so that they could be drained in a process known as "hot tapping." As described by the commander of the operation, Lt. Cdr. Tim Emge: "Hot tapping allows us to safely tie into the many tanks without leakage by creating a secure opening to place the valve, hot tap tool and pipe for pumping from the highest point on the tank. . . . We were able to successfully, and most importantly safely, conduct over a hundred hot taps throughout the operation."

In this process the divers removed 250,000 gallons of fuel oil (1,025 tons) stored in the ship's 159 external tanks distributed along the hull wall and 14 interior tanks. The job was completed on 15 October. The remaining oil was sealed in interior tanks where the salvage crew considered it secure from leaking.

Prinz Eugen's wreck in 2014. It is a popular dive site, but in 2014 her bunkers still have oil, and she is considered at extreme risk of polluting the lagoon. (U.S. Fish and Wildlife Service)

Today *Prinz Eugen* still lies where she was stranded 200 yards off Enubuj (Carlson) Islet 3.6 miles from Kwajalein pier and four miles from Ebeye, the atoll's major population center. The wreck is a popular dive site. Reportedly two turrets and several 10.5-cm guns are still intact, and the port torpedo tubes still have torpedoes inside. The interior structures are accessible, but several divers have lost their lives while exploring inside. According to a description from *X-Ray* magazine:

Prinz Eugen's propeller on display at the Laboe Naval Memorial near Kiel. (Public Domain)

Several doorways can be used to enter the inside of the wreck. A dive into these openings leads through rusty red alleys. These old walls move slowly and statically back and forth driven by the current. It is a strange ghostly scene. Navigation demands concentration due to the fact that the wreck is lying upside down. Beds are mounted to the "ceiling." Divers can penetrate deeper into the wreck while moving along white ropes that were brought in years ago. Several sections of the wreck can be explored: galleys, storage rooms, bathrooms, generators, different types of shelves—more and more relics appear in the light of the torch. The officer's rooms have chairs, tables and beds. Everything is buried under several inches of rust.

The story of *Prinz Eugen* is clearly not yet ended, even though the role she fills today is far different than originally intended.

Recovery efforts showing USNS *Salvor* and *Humber* anchored over the wreck of *Prinz Eugen*. (U.S. Navy)

Divers hot-tapping the exterior oil tanks on *Prinz Eugen* by drilling through the hull. (U.S. Navy)

USNS *Salvor*, a salvage and rescue vessel operated by the Military Sealift Command. She was commissioned in 1986. This photo was taken off Singapore in 2006.

World of Warships is a free-to-play naval warfare-themed massively multiplayer online game produced and published by Wargaming. Like their other games, *World of Tanks* (WoT) and *World of Warplanes* (WoWP); players take control of historic vehicles to battle others in player-vs-player or play cooperatively against bots or in a player versus environment (PvE) battle mode. *World of Warships* (WoWs) was originally released for on PC in 2015, the PlayStation 4 and Xbox One console versions, titled *World of Warships: Legends*, followed in 2019 and released on the PlayStation 5 and Xbox Series X/S in April 2021.

Developed by Lesta Studios in St. Petersburg Russia, *World of Warships* (PC) currently has over 44 million registered players – playing on five main servers across the globe. Over 500 dedicated staff members work on a four-week update cycle to bring new features, ships, and mechanics to the game – keeping game play fresh and inviting to new players. The game features over 400 ships, spread across 12 different in game nations. Ships are designed based on historical documents and actual blueprints from the first half of the 20th century, and it takes from two to six man-months on average to create each of these ships. There are over 20 ports to choose from, and 10 of them are recreated based on historical harbors and port towns.

There are four different ship classes: destroyers, cruisers, battleships, and aircraft carriers; with each class offering a different gameplay experience. Submarines have been in testing cycles since 2018, based on testing results and players' feedback then they have undergone significant changes that should allow them to launch as the fifth class in the near future. Ships are arranged in tiers between I and X, players must progress through ship classes and tiers to reach tier X. Ships of tier X represent the pinnacle of naval engineering from World War II and the early Cold War era. Each warship needs a naval commander to lead it into the battle. There are many commanders to choose from in World of Warships, including over 10 iconic historical figures. In World of Warships players can battle on more than 40 maps. There are seven different permanent or seasonal Battle Types to choose from: Co-op Battles, Random Battles, Ranked Battles, Clan Battles, Brawls, Scenarios and Training. From time-to-time additional Event battles are held. Additionally, within Battle Types there are four different Battle Modes available: Standard, Domination, Epicenter and Arms Race.

Prinz Eugen made her *World of Warships* PC debut as a Promotional Premium German tier VIII and was met with mixed reviews. Although having a better gun reload than her tech tree sister, *Admiral Hipper*, the two ships were fundamentally the same. Once made purchasable in the premium store and given the repair party consumable – *Prinz Eugen* was able to stand out as a reliable tier VIII premium cruiser. Her great health pool, average armor, fast speed, and variety of armaments and consumables make her a formidable opponent. Like other German cruisers, her main gun AP shell performance is excellent but trades for poor HE shell performance. Excellent hydroacoustic search, a decent AA battery, and quadruple triple-torpedo launchers make her an excellent all-rounder. Pick *Prinz Eugen* up in the premium shop and sail her into battle in *World of Warships* and *World of Warships: Legends* today!

Developed by the team behind *World of Warships* for PC, *World of Warships: Legends* is a completely new entry in Wargaming's flagship nautical franchise that takes full advantage of the power and capabilities of home consoles. *World of Warships: Legends* brings the online naval action loved by millions to home consoles for the very first time, alongside a host of content and features exclusive to the console experience. *World of Warships: Legends* is now available to download from the PlayStation® Store and Microsoft Store. Players can now wage wars across

a variety of maps, in numerous warships and enjoy stunning oceanic vistas with glorious HDR support on PlayStation®4 and Xbox One X. Full 4K support is available on PlayStation®4 Pro and PlayStation®5, Xbox One X too! *Legends* also supports standard high-def on PlayStation®4 and Xbox One with more intriguing graphics on the horizon.

Wargaming proudly supports various charitable causes that members of the gaming and history community deeply care for. Supporting veterans and servicemembers: Operation Lifeboat (2020) raised $150,000 USD for Stack Up's mental health awareness helpline, Remembrance charity drive (2020) raised $45,000 USD for Help for Heroes, who supports UK veterans and service members, and Project Valor (2017) saw WoWS, WoT, and WoWP collectively raising $75,000 USD for a veteran housing program. Preserving historical ship museums: *World of Warships* partners with museums across the world to support the preservation of naval history and the education of the global community, with $50,000 USD raised for the restoration of USS *Batfish* (2019) and $400,000 USD raised for the restoration of USS *Texas* (2017). Finally, supporting the local community: a 24-hour charity livestream (2019) raised $43,000 USD for the Save the Children organization, and $78,000 USD for Team Rubicon and the victims of Hurricane Harvey in 2017.

The United States Naval Institute (USNI) has been a proud partner of *World of Warships* and Wargaming since December of 2019. Wargaming has a made a commitment to naval history through various programs and events of over the past years. They produce excellent video

Prinz Eugen was an **Admiral Hipper**–class heavy cruiser that entered service in 1940. The ship's badge includes elements from the Coat of Arms of the famous Prince Eugene of Savoy, the Austrian commander of the late 17th-early 18th centuries, whose name the ship bears.

content with their *Naval Legends* series on YouTube, and host events aboard museum ships where members of the gaming and naval history community can get together and experience the living-history in person. *World of Warships* and Wargaming are also great sponsors of HNSA (Historic Naval Ships Association). USNI thanks Wargaming and *World of Warships* for their continued support of the naval history community and participation in this *Naval History Special Edition*. Please see the back cover for a special offer for *World of Warships* PC and *World of Warships: Legends*.

Admiral Hipper franz von Hipper

Franz von Hipper (1863–1932) was an admiral in the German Imperial Navy (1918). In 1913, Hipper distinguished himself when he commanded the First Scouting Group, consisting of powerful high-speed battlecruisers. Hipper's squadron took part in the two largest naval battles of World War I—the Battle of Dogger Bank in January 1915, and the Battle of Jutland in May and June 1916.

Owing to the admiral's decisive and skillful actions, as well as the impeccable accuracy of his cruisers when firing, the reconnaissance forces of the High Seas Fleet gracefully managed to cope with any situation, even when facing more powerful opposition. The most painful losses of the British during the Battle of Jutland—three battlecruisers—were caused by Admiral Hipper's squadron. In April 1939, *Admiral Hipper*, the lead ship in a series of five heavy cruisers, joined the German Navy. *Prinz Eugen* would become the third and last ship of the class, with the fourth hull being sold to the Soviet Union and the fifth being canceled.

A bid for the development of a new reconnaissance seaplane to replace the obsolete He 60 for the Kriegsmarine was announced in 1936. In 1937, the bidders underwent various tests, and the winner was a monoplane designated "AR 196," developed by the Arado company.

In 1938, the first ship to take the new aircraft on board was the "pocket battleship" *Admiral Graf Spee*. The extremely successful and well-armed AR 196 became the most-produced German seaplane of its time. During the war, these aircraft were used all the way from the Arctic to the South Atlantic and were deservedly known as the "eyes of the Kriegsmarine."

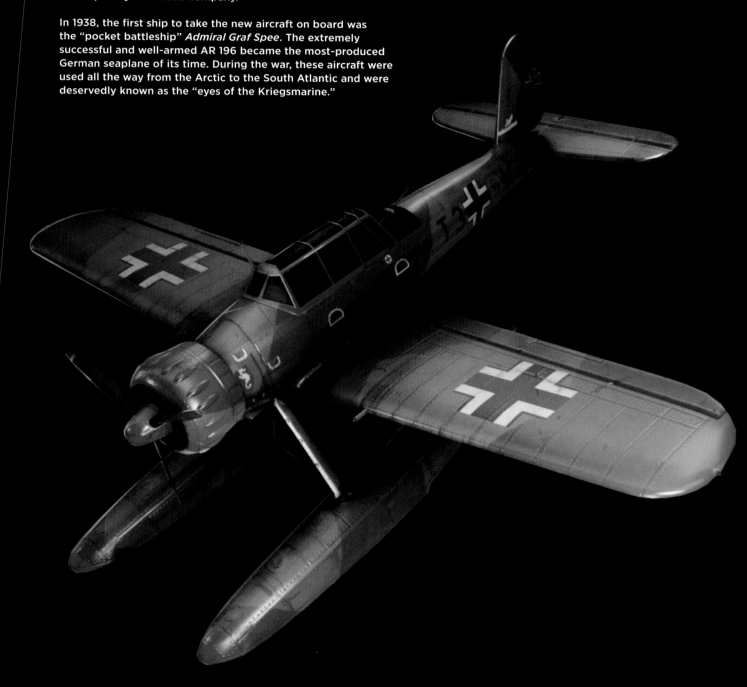

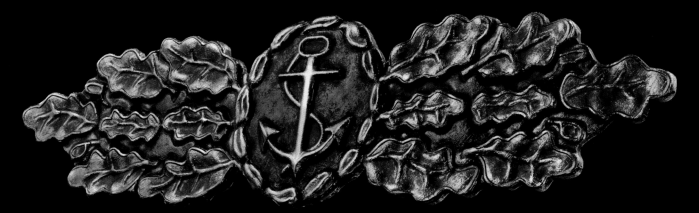

This badge was introduced on 19 November 1944 for all Kriegsmarine servicemen, except those who served on submarines who had already been given an award of similar quality. It was created based on the Close Combat Clasp award of the Wehrmacht, which was given to the best and most experienced veterans. It was worn above the left breast pocket.

The badge was awarded to those who had already received a regular war badge five times—this was an award for long honorable service under combat conditions. Given that the war badge was introduced at the end of the war, the number of those who received it is unknown.

Naval Institute Press publications you might enjoy:

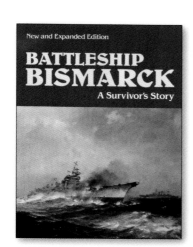

978-1-55750-436-4

Paperback | 📖

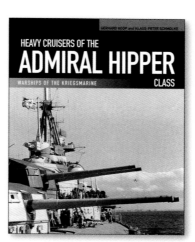

978-1-59114-168-6

Paperback | 📖

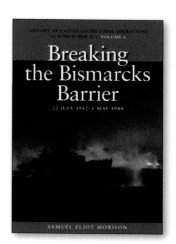

978-1-59114-552-3

Paperback

Naval History Special Editions

8½ x 10¾ | Paperback | **$19.95**

Building upon the expertise of the authors and historians of the Naval Institute Press, the *Naval History* Special Editions are designed to offer studies of the key vessels, battles, and events of armed conflict. Using an image-heavy, magazine-style format, these Special Editions should appeal to scholars, enthusiasts, and general readers alike.

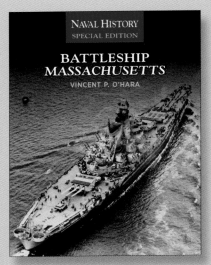

Battleship *Massachusetts*

BY VINCENT P. O'HARA
978-1-68247-635-2

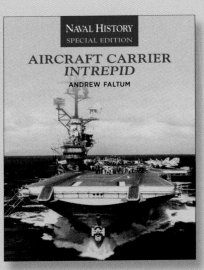

Aircraft Carrier *Intrepid*

BY ANDREW FALTUM
978-1-68247-740-3

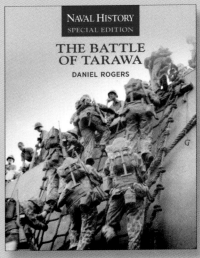

The Battle of Tarawa

BY DANIEL ROGERS
978-1-59114-703-9

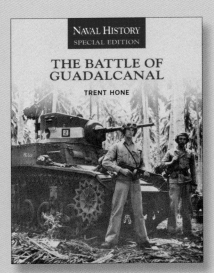

The Battle of Guadalcanal

BY TRENT HONE
978-1-68247-731-1

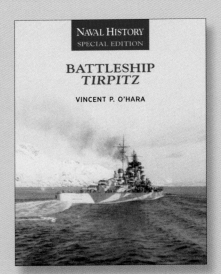

Battleship *Tirpitz*

BY VINCENT P. O'HARA
978-1-59114-870-8

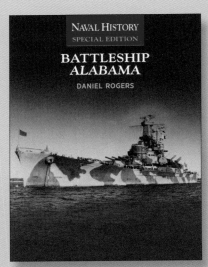

Battleship *Alabama*

BY DANIEL ROGERS
978-1-59114-698-8

UNITED STATES NAVAL INSTITUTE